A New Vision for Iowa
Food and Agriculture

A New Vision for Iowa Food and Agriculture

Francis Thicke, PhD

Mulberry Knoll

Interior design & production by Allen Cobb.

Printed in the United States of America.
First printing June 2010.
Second printing July 2010.
10 9 8 7 6 5 4 3

ISBN-13: 978-0-9792104-0-2
ISBN-10: 0-9792104-0-2

To contact the author, please write to:
    Francis Thicke
    1745 Brookville Rd
    Fairfield, IA 52556

Or email:
    fthicke@iowatelecom.net

Mulberry Knoll Books
Fairfield, Iowa, USA
info@MulberryKnoll.com

DEDICATION

To Susan Noll Thicke

Contents

Energy Solutions for Agriculture

Local and Regional Food Systems

Acknowledgements

To write a book while running a dairy farm, processing milk on the farm, and campaigning for public office has been quite a challenge. It would not have been
possible without the help and forbearance of many
people. First I want to thank Rodney Tedrow, who lives
on our farm with his wife, Jill. Rodney has stepped up
and become a dairy farmer in short order, allowing me
to feel confident that when I travel, the cows will be
taken care of and the normal "emergencies" of farming
will be handled (but I keep my cell phone turned on).
Rodney shares my philosophy that farming should be
a fun and creative adventure. Thanks also to the whole
farm and dairy processing crew: Jeanine, Kim, Rich-
ard, Uriah, and Gabrielle.

I thank Bill Witherspoon and the folks at the Sustainable Research Institute for their support and encouragement to undertake this project, without which this
book would not have happened. Thanks to George
and Mary Foster for creating the book cover and Allen
Cobb for designing and producing the book interior.
Thanks to Rob Hubler for his constant encouragement
to get the book finished, and for his understanding
when it wasn't. John Day, Leon Lewis, Bob Ferguson,
Ed Malloy, and Arthur Lee Land have also each contributed in their own special ways.

sign" or "be forced to change by default." There is little we can do about the changes coming at us—the end of cheap energy, climate destabilization, depleting fresh water resources—but we can begin preparing for them.

Thicke is concerned about the fact that most of us in Iowa tend to be oblivious to these changes. Yet, that is probably to be expected. No one likes change. We would all prefer to continue doing what we know best. Understandably, we especially tend to be reluctant to change when we have made huge investments in our current business enterprises, as we have in our food and agriculture ventures. Whether we are farmers, food processors, agricultural input suppliers or food distributors and retailers, we would all rather continue with business as usual. Additionally, we are especially reluctant to change when we have reached the end of our careers, as many farmers have. More than 30 percent of U.S. farmers are now over age 65.

But, Francis is keenly aware of the fact that challenges also present us with opportunities and some of those opportunities in agriculture have the potential to stimulate the economy, restore the resilience of our ecologies and revitalize our rural communities. That is the future Francis envisions for Iowa and one to which he is dedicating himself.

Francis reminds us that in our time, we are already moving from an industrial age to an information age. And, with respect to agriculture, he believes it will be especially important that this transition be guided by a "holistic" rather than a "reductionist" information model. Agriculture is ultimately a biological enterprise, but throughout the industrial era, we largely ignored the natural biological resources of agriculture because cheap energy allowed us to invent and implement energy intensive technological substitutes that seemed much more effective. But, as cheap energy disappears from the landscape, a transition from an energy intensive system to a knowledge intensive system (grounded in the science of ecology) will become critical. That means we will have to fundamentally redesign our agricultural systems, not simply invent new technologies to bolster our current industrial system.

Francis provides a compelling example in his analysis of methane digesters. While investing in methane digesters has the potential to produce energy on the farm and reduce methane emissions, it fails to recognize that methane digesters will require that animals continue to be kept in confinement to collect their manure. That means the energy intensive industrial system has to be maintained—a highly questionable proposition once cheap energy is no longer available. Consequently, alternative, ecologically designed systems of production will be a more viable option in the future, and Thicke provides us with many practical examples of such alternatives.

Thicke's vision for Iowa agriculture is informed by his own experience as a farmer and by his academic study and research. Of course, not everyone will agree with his vision for the future of Iowa agriculture. That is to be expected. Such disagreements are a normal part of cultural transformations. And I know Francis well enough to know that he will welcome alternative suggestions so long as they address the central question: How do we prepare for our new future so that the changes coming at us can be "peaceful and orderly" and Iowa's agriculture can be a model of sustainable production? We have the opportunity in the decades ahead to design an agriculture that can be more economically, socially, and ecologically resilient. That is the future to which Francis has dedicated himself— and so should we.

Frederick Kirschenmann

Distinguished Fellow,
Leopold Center for Sustainable Agriculture.

President,
Stone Barns Center for Food and Agriculture.

Introduction

Iowa has a long, proud tradition of being a leader in agriculture. The Iowa prairies have bestowed on us some of the richest, deepest soils in the world. We have a good temperate climate that is conducive to good crop production. And we have a strong tradition of hardworking people in Iowa. All of these things have made Iowa an agricultural powerhouse, a shining jewel among agricultural states.

But now we are in a time of great change. Iowa agriculture is facing some major challenges and will need to change if it is to thrive in these changing times. Unfortunately, some of the challenges we face are little discussed or even acknowledged today. Also little noticed are some of the more exceptional opportunities for new directions in agriculture that are on the horizon today. We can capitalize on these opportunities to help us meet and surmount the challenges we face.

Climate scientists tell us that our climate is changing, and we should expect a growing frequency of extreme weather events. We have already seen that manifesting as intense rainfall and severe flooding. The flood of 2008 caused tremendous damage in Iowa, including soil erosion rates of 20 tons per acre on ten percent of

Iowa's cropland, which is nearly five times the amount of soil normally lost in the course of a year.

Our dominant cropping systems in Iowa are not resilient enough to withstand such weather extremes. Already, our environment has been compromised by farming practices of the past. Since we began cropping Iowa's soils, half of our original topsoil has been lost or moved by erosion. And, half of the original organic matter—the heart of our deep, fertile soil—has been lost. We cannot continue on this path of deficit spending of the ecological capital that the prairies bequeathed us.

We have water quality problems in Iowa for which agriculture must take some responsibility. We also have problems caused by Concentrated Animal Feeding Operations (CAFOs). They are a source of great divisiveness in rural Iowa, compromising our air and water quality, our property values, our quality of life, and even the health of Iowa citizens.

Agribusiness corporations are monopolizing agricultural markets and usurping profits that should rightly go to farmers. We have lost connection with our food, which travels great distances to get to our dinner plate. We have a crisis of obesity and diet-related health problems.

Probably the biggest challenge we are facing today is that we have an agriculture that is highly dependent on cheap fossil fuels in a world of escalating fossil-fuel prices. Without cheap oil, our current agriculture and food system will become imperiled and may fail us. Yet, we seem oblivious to how we are going to power agriculture in the future. We are making ethanol for cars driving on highways, but have done virtually nothing to secure the energy future of Iowa agriculture.

The good news is that there are exciting solutions on the horizon for all these challenges we face. Some of the opportunities we can use to help us meet these challenges include:

- More biodiversity on the landscape

- Integration of livestock onto the landscape

- Greater use of perennial and cover cropping systems

- Perennial crops for biofuel production

- Greater energy efficiency of agriculture

- Powering farms with farm-scale wind, solar, and biofuel production systems

- Breaking up agribusiness monopolies and restoring competition to agricultural markets

- Local control and tightened regulation of CAFOs

- Increased local food production

To meet the challenges of the 21st Century will require new vision and new leadership. Iowa agriculture could lead Iowa and the nation to a new economy based on sustainable renewable energy, environmentally sound farming systems and thriving rural communities. However, continuing on the path of the status quo will not get us there. What will be required is a clear vision of the future we want to create, creative planning and policy making, commitment to research and development of appropriate technologies, and firm resolve to carry us through.

Section I

Industrial Agriculture vs. Ecological Agriculture

1

From the Industrial Revolution to Industrial Agriculture: The Road to CAFOs

The Industrial Revolution began in England more than 250 years ago. Newly invented machinery began producing goods that had previously been made by hand.[1] Soon it was discovered that grouping the machines in buildings greatly increased production efficiency and output. The creation of the factory marked the beginning of a trend toward factory manufacturing of goods that had previously been produced in homes or by groups of artisans.

It also was the beginning of the transformation of society as industry began to dominate the socioeconomic order. The Industrial Revolution brought economic development, but also profoundly changed the social order. Factory owners, who needed cheap, unskilled labor, profited greatly by using children and women to run the machines. By the age of 6, many children were working 14 hours a day in factories.[2] Fortunately, over time, with the advent of labor unions and social advocacy, factory working conditions improved greatly.

Industrialization did not overtake agriculture as quickly as it did some other areas of production, such as textiles and printing. No doubt, that was because agriculture was intimately connected with nature's ecology for its production. Nature's ecology—with its dependence on weather, soil, and the interactions of many organisms—was not so easily controlled and converted to a factory process.

Changes in agriculture came gradually for the first 200 years of the Industrial Revolution. First, wooden farm implements were replaced by iron ones. Early on, Jethro Tull invented the seed drill and horse hoe, which made preparing a seed bed and planting easier. Eli Whitney invented the cotton gin in 1793. Cyprus McCormick patented the mechanical grain reaper in 1834. In 1854, the first self-governing windmill was perfected. John Deere began manufacturing steel plows in 1837, the same year that the first practical threshing machine was patented. In the early 1900s, the first practical tractors came into use. All of these innovations helped ease the work of farming but did not radically transform agriculture. Farms, for the most part, remained diversified operations that raised a variety of crops and livestock.

The close of World War II made new tools widely available to accelerate the industrialization of crop production. This in turn led the way to industrialized animal production. Factories that had been producing explosives and chemical weapons for the war effort were suddenly idled when the war ended. Coincidentally, factories that had made explosives could be converted to making nitrogen fertilizer, and chemicals developed during the war were found to be effective as pesticides.[3] Another important factor that accelerated the trend toward industrial farming was the availability of cheap fossil fuels to power farm machinery and to make farm chemicals. Undoubtedly, cheap fossil fuels played a key role in the industrialization of agriculture.

Armed with inexpensive synthetic fertilizers, herbicides, insecticides, fungicides, and fuel, American farmers began to change farming practices. They abandoned crop rotations that formerly had been used to boost soil fertility and reduce infestations of weeds, insects, and pathogens. They increasingly turned to monoculture of a few annual crops. The advent of farm subsidy programs that paid farmers to grow just a few commodity crops also contributed to the loss of crop diversity. In 1920, 34 commodities (crop and animal enterprises) were produced for sale on at least 1 percent of Iowa farms. By 1997, only 10 commodities were produced for sale on 1 percent of Iowa farms.[4]

With the industrialization of crop production, animal manures were replaced with synthetic fertilizers. Consequently, crop farms could achieve high production without animals. The availability of cheap synthetic fertilizers meant that animal manures began to be considered more of a nuisance than a resource. That view overlooked the value of organic carbon—present in manure but lacking in synthetic fertilizers—with the long-term consequence of contributing to the reduction of soil organic carbon, what you might call a "de-sequestering" of soil carbon. Soil microorganisms use organic carbon as a food source. If less organic carbon —such as is present in animal manure or crop residue —is added to the soil on a regular basis, soil carbon levels will decline over time. Tillage also contributes to a decline in soil organic matter levels, as does nitrogen fertilizer use.[5]

Livestock production became increasingly separated from crop production. The size and concentration of livestock operations grew, and livestock production facilities began increasingly to resemble factories. Today, advocates for concentrated animal feeding operations (CAFOs) reject the term "factory farm" as pejorative. However, it is the factory-like design of CAFOs, where conditions of production are tightly controlled, that is the chief appeal and selling point for confinement animal production.

2

The Information Age: The Path toward Ecological Crop and Livestock Production

The wave of industrialization that ushered animals into CAFOs in industrialized countries didn't begin in earnest until the latter part of the 20ᵗʰ Century. This is the same timeframe within which modern society began its transition out of the Industrial Age and into the Information Age.[6] That means that CAFOs—the epitome of industrial livestock production—came into vogue just in time to be obsolete, just as society was transitioning from an industrial mode to knowledge-based systems.

What does the Information Age mean for agriculture? It means a vast expansion of scientific knowledge about plants, animals, and soils—and the web of connections and interactions among them. In short, the Information Age is bringing agriculture a deeper understanding of nature's ecology. Armed with this deeper knowledge of the ecology of crops, soils, weeds, insects, and other pathogens, we are now in a position to design and manage crop and livestock systems that mimic the functions of natural ecologies. By using ecology as a model, we can strategically use crop rotations, beneficial insects, cover crops, nitrogen-fixing crops, managed grazing and other practices to circumvent the need for herbicides, pesticides, fertilizers, and fossil-fuel energy. This ecology-based approach to agriculture will help us protect and improve soil quality, water quality, air quality and wildlife habitat. A good example of an ecologically designed animal production system is a grass-based dairy farm, which will be explored in detail below.

Wikipedia describes the transition from the Industrial Age to the Information Age as "a shift from traditional industry that the Industrial Revolution brought through industrialization, to an economy based around the manipulation of information."[7] For livestock production, that shift means a shift from industrial CAFO-style systems to production systems that use information to harness the efficiency, energy, and organizing power of nature's ecology in the design and management of animal production systems.

It is important to distinguish between holistic uses of information—in which the many interactions of the parts of a system and the system's effect on its external environment are taken into account—and a reductionist approach to information. Reductionism refers to the theory that a complex system can be fully understood by understanding the components of the system. In a reductionist approach, the functions of the parts of a system are optimized but less consideration is given to the holistic function of the system and the system's effect on the surrounding environment.

For example, the design and management of animal confinement systems are certainly based on a lot of technical information, such as the mechanics of how to house and feed as many animals as possible in as little space as possible, and how to use pharmaceuticals to overcome disease pressures in closely confined animals. That reductionist approach, however, ignores the holistic understanding of natural animal behaviors that are thwarted by close confinement and the health problems that may be caused or aggravated by such close confinement. A more holistic, or ecological, approach to animal husbandry takes into account that animals can be healthier—and fewer pharmaceuticals may be needed—if animals are less crowded and in a more natural environment.

The differences between reductionist and holistic applications of information can also be seen in crop production systems. For example, a reductionist approach reveals that high yields and profits may be obtained by continuously growing annual crops (such as corn and soybeans) using high fertilizer rates, and tile drainage systems under the soil to remove excess water. However, that ignores the holistic (ecological) understanding that such a system inherently leaks nitrate into water resources and is prone to excessive soil erosion.

The reductionist attempt to solve the problem of soil erosion in annual crop production is to build more terraces and other mechanical structures to try to slow down water runoff in order to reduce its erosive power. The reductionist approach to solving the problem of nitrate leaching from the soil in annual crop production is to build artificial wetlands below tile drainage lines to try to remove the leached nitrate from the water before it gets into the river. A holistic, or ecological, solution to both soil erosion and nitrate leaching is to use more cover and perennial crops in the crop rotation, which reduces both soil erosion and nitrate leaching.

Genetic engineering of crops also tends to follow a reductionist approach. Engineering a crop to be able to withstand the herbicide glyphosate—which will kill all other plants—produces good weed control (at least initially). However, unintended consequences of this reductionist approach to weed control include the evolution of weeds that become resistant to glyphosate,[8] concerns about glyphosate toxicity for non-target species such as amphibians,[9] human health concerns about genetically modified foods,[10] [11] and unintended effects of glyphosate on soil microbiology and crop performance.[12]

An example of a more holistic, ecological approach to weed control is some promising new research on the use of cover crops for weed control.[13] In this system, a cover crop is planted in the fall and the following spring the cover crop is flattened and killed with a roller/crimper tool. A crop is then planted into the rolled-down residue. The cover crop residue keeps weeds from growing, helps retain soil moisture, feeds soil microorganisms and contributes to carbon sequestration in the soil.

For agriculture, the Information Age should be called the Age of Ecology or the Knowledge Age, where knowledge refers to holistic, integrated use of information.

Another harbinger of the coming transition to ecologically based agricultural systems is the escalating cost of fossil-fuel energy. Energy costs are a growing burden for industrial agriculture. The industrial system of agriculture we have today could not have developed without cheap fossil-fuel energy, and it will not likely be able to survive the prohibitively expensive fossil fuels of tomorrow.

The end of the cheap-fossil-fuel era in agriculture presents us with two choices: to change our agricultural systems through foresight, planning, and design, or to be forced to change by default when agriculture gets priced out of the fossil-fuel market. If we wait until agriculture is priced out of the fossil-fuel market before beginning to transition to a post-fossil-fuel agriculture, we will undoubtedly experience chaos and hardship, and possibly food shortages. The sudden oil price spike of 2008 was a lesson in how quickly and unexpectedly high oil prices can rise. If oil economist Jeff Rubin is right, the future will bring us a roller coaster of oil-price ups and downs, with increasingly higher price spikes.[14]

The coming transition to an agriculture that is not dependent on fossil fuels presents an opportunity to re-create our agriculture so it becomes more profitable for family farmers, supports thriving rural communities, and better protects the environment.

3

Factory Farms vs. Family Farms

The term CAFO is commonly used to refer to any animal confinement facility. However, CAFO has a legal definition. Under the federal Clean Water Act, the term CAFO means Concentrated (not confined) Animal Feeding Operation and is defined as an animal feeding operation of more than 1000 animal units.[15] A thousand animal units is equivalent to 1000 beef cows, 700 dairy cows, 2500 pigs weighing more than 55 pounds, 125,000 broiler chickens, or 82,000 laying hens. The term CAFO applies to both open feedlots and animal confinement buildings that meet these minimum size requirements.

As mentioned above, the term "factory farm" is now considered to be pejorative. Advocates for animal confinement systems often challenge their detractors to define exactly what a factory farm is and how it differs from a family farm. However, unlike the term "CAFO," which is legally defined by the Clean Water Act, factory farms and family farms do not have such precise definitions.

Dictionary.com's 21st Century Lexicon defines a factory farm as "a system of large-scale industrialized and intensive agriculture that is focused on profit with animals kept indoors and restricted in mobility."[16] While that definition is descriptive, it lacks precision and excludes large outdoor feedlots, which are included in the federal legal definition of CAFOs, and which many would argue are outdoor factory farms.

Obviously, a family can own a factory farm, just as a family can own any other type of factory. But does family ownership make a CAFO a family farm? The National Coalition of Family Farmers (NCFF) argues that it does not; rather, the source of a farm's management and labor are key to defining a family farm: "A family farm is not defined by size, but rather by the fact that the family provides the vast majority of the labor and management decisions."[17]

Most large CAFOs would not fit NCFF's definition of a family farm because they are either completely owned by large corporations, or the animals, feed, and management are under corporate ownership. The farmer who houses the animals is paid on a contract basis. According to a study by USDA's Economic Research Service, as of 2004, less than a third of U.S. hogs were independently owned and marketed by farmers.[18]

4

Economics of CAFOs

Research at the University of Wisconsin has found that grass-based dairies have lower costs ($650 less per cow) and greater profits ($230 more per cow) than CAFO dairies.[19] As energy costs continue to rise, grass-based livestock systems will likely become increasingly more profitable relative to CAFO systems. That is because in grass-based livestock systems, the animals harvest their own feed and spread their own manure, eliminating the energy costs associated with having to perform those functions mechanically.

Research in Iowa[20] and North Dakota[21] has found that on a per-hog basis the profitability of raising hogs in pasture-based systems or in deep-bedded hoop houses—two alternatives to CAFOs—is about the same as raising hogs in CAFOs. So, why aren't more hogs raised in hoop houses or pasture instead of in confinement buildings? Most hogs are raised under contract with corporations that determine how the pigs are to be raised. For the contracting corporations, it is easier to deal with large CAFOs because that makes it easier to control for uniform growing conditions and to pick up large lots of finished hogs. Independent hog production (and beef production) is becoming increasingly rare as markets become more concentrated and independent producers lose their ability to compete in a market dominated by large players.

In contract hog production, corporate contractors—called integrators—own the hogs and provide the feed for the hogs. Farmer contractees are paid on a per-hog basis and are required to build and own the CAFO buildings and dispose of the manure. Growing hogs on a contract basis provides farmers with a guaranteed income and isolates them from the risks of fluctuating market prices. But it also locks farmers out of high profits when market prices are high. In the long run, under contract hog production, more profits go to corporate coffers instead of staying on the farm and in the community. The net effect is that contract hog production reduces the number of farmers on the land, which reduces the population and viability of rural communities. In 1978, there were 59,000 Iowa farms raising pigs. By 2002, just 10,000 Iowa farms raised pigs.[22] That is more than an 80 percent drop in Iowa farms raising pigs over 25 years.

A further problem with the structure in which farmers raise hogs on contract with outside corporations is that farmers have little negotiating power over the terms of their contracts. As hog ownership becomes increasingly concentrated in the hands of fewer and larger corporations, farmers have fewer contract options. Corporations have more power to reduce contract rates or cancel contracts altogether to suit their corporate business plan. That leaves farmers—who have the financial obligations to pay debts on CAFO buildings—in a precarious position. There were reports that in 2009, some Iowa farmers who were raising hogs on contract had their contracts cancelled when the hog market took a downturn.[23] Other farmers were forced to renegotiate the terms of their contracts, making them even less profitable.

This same scenario has played out in the past with poultry CAFO production in the southeastern United States. Initially, poultry farmers were offered attractive contracts to raise poultry for integrators. When the poultry CAFO industry matured to the point that there were more poultry CAFOs than were needed, the integrators reduced the terms of their contracts with farmers and threatened to cancel contracts unless farmers continued to meet their demands for expensive upgrades to CAFO facilities[24]. As a result, contract poultry production pays a meager return to farmers today, and much of the wealth created by poultry production is being extracted from farms and local communities.

5

Market Concentration

A growing problem in today's agriculture—that reduces profits returned to farmers—is the increasing concentration of market power in the hands of a few corporations. Economists tell us that when four corporations control 40 percent or more of a market, that market loses its competitive nature and begins to take on the characteristics of a monopoly.[25] As of 2007, four corporations control 84 percent of the beef packer market; four corporations control 66 percent of the pork packer market; four corporations control 59 percent of the broiler market.[26] The turkey, flour milling, seed, and other agricultural markets are similarly concentrated.

The effects on farmers of the growing concentration of food processing markets are further accentuated by the increasing consolidation and concentration of the retail food market. "Big-box" grocery store chains have gained the power to dictate wholesale prices to food processors. That forces food processors in turn to reduce their transactional costs. One way to do that is to try to do business exclusively with large farmers. It is cheaper to buy 10,000 hogs from one farmer than to buy 1,000 hogs from each of 10 farmers.

In addition to the effects of market concentration, the system of vertical integration of markets by large corporations can also distort market conditions and reduce profits returned to farmers. Vertical integration refers to a company owning a commodity all the way through the food chain—from production, through marketing, to retailing. For example, if a corporation owns large numbers of hogs from farrowing (birth) through finishing to market weight, through processing and wholesaling of the meat, that corporation is in a position to use some discretion in how it allocates its overall profits within the various market segments. If that corporation were a dominant player in the market, it could allocate more profits to the processing and wholesale segments of the market and less to the hog production segment. That would depress market prices of hogs for independent producers selling into the same market but would not affect the overall profits of the vertically integrated corporation.

The anticompetitive effects of market concentration are further compounded by the prevalence of horizontal integration. Today several of the top four corporations in each concentrated market category are also among the top four corporations in other concentrated markets. For example, Tyson is No. 1 in beef packing, No. 2 in pork packing and No. 2 in broilers. This kind of horizontal integration encourages corporations that dominate in several markets to manipulate prices in order to increase their market share. For example, when beef and broiler prices are profitable, a corporation with dominant market share in beef, broilers, and pork can take measures to create and prolong unprofitable conditions in the pork market in order to force out other companies that deal only in pork. Meanwhile, the company that is horizontally integrated can maintain its own overall corporate profitability through the beef and broiler market sectors.

A recent example of the effect of market concentration on farmer profitability is what happened in the milk market in 2009. Dairy farmers experienced record losses due to low farm-level milk prices. At the same time, the largest dairy processor, Dean Foods—which purportedly controls 40 percent of U.S. dairy processing—posted record quarterly profits.[27] Apparently, Dean Foods has found a *modus operandi* that enables it to achieve record high profits on its processed dairy products at the same time that dairy farmers receive record low prices for the milk that is used to make those dairy products.

In the past 15 years, Dean Foods has bought up more than 100 previously independent dairy processing plants.[28] Dean Foods has powers of both horizontal and vertical integration. In 2008, it had net sales of $12.5 billion[29] from a wide range of dairy products under many major brand names. Dean Foods is also the largest U.S. producer of both soy milk and organic milk.

In 2010, after many years of ignoring the growing market power of Dean Foods and many other companies that dominate agricultural markets, the U.S. Justice Department filed an antitrust suit against Dean Foods. The suit is seeking to overturn Dean Foods' acquisition of two Midwest dairy processing plants. With those acquisitions, Dean Foods controlled 57 percent of the Midwestern regional dairy market, according to the Department of Justice.

What we need today is Teddy Roosevelt-style trust-busting to break up the oligarchy control of agricultural markets. Presidential administrations of recent decades have done little to nothing to stop the rapid consolidation of agricultural markets. However, the Obama Administration has promised to investigate the effects of concentrated market power on competition in agriculture. That provides a ray of hope, but it will take aggressive actions to break up monopoly power and bring competition back to agricultural markets.

6

Industrial Agriculture vs. Nature's Ecology

The term "sustainable agriculture" has become widely used in the farm press. It is defined in a variety of ways and increasingly it is being co-opted by advocates for conventional agriculture to greenwash the industrial approach to agriculture. For example, the Monsanto Corporation calls their marketing program to dominate the world seed market "sustainable agriculture."[30]

Many definitions of sustainable agriculture used today include several common elements. According to those definitions, to be sustainable, agriculture must be 1) economically viable, 2) ecologically sound, 3) socially responsible, and 4) humane.

Because sustainable agriculture has been defined in many ways and co-opted by agribusiness industries, I find the term "ecological agriculture" more useful for describing the antithesis of industrial agriculture. It can be an instructive exercise to contrast the biologically based, integrated organization of a natural ecology with the reductionist design of industrial agricultural systems. Then we can consider how we might design agricultural systems to utilize the efficiencies and organizing power of nature's ecology. The table below contrasts some of the characteristics of a natural ecology with opposing characteristics of industrial agriculture.

Natural Ecology	Industrial Agriculture
Biodiversity	Monoculture
Self-Regulatory	Dependence on Herbicides, Pesticides, Fertilizers
Energy Efficiency	Dependence on Fossil Fuels
Self-Renewing	Depletion of Ecological Capital
Resilient	Vulnerable to Resource Impairment
Recycling	Leakage of Pollutants

Characteristics of a natural ecology compared to industrial agriculture.

In industrial agriculture, monoculture replaces the biodiversity of a natural ecosystem. We are accustomed to seeing monoculture crop systems—vast expanses of corn or soybeans, for example. What may be less obvious (because much of it happens indoors) is that industrial livestock production is also a monoculture system, in which many animals of a single species are confined together in isolation from the biological diversity found in their natural environments.

To maintain a monoculture requires energy and other fossil-fuel-based inputs, in contrast to the recycling and system self renewal inherent in a natural ecology. For example, to grow monoculture corn requires herbicides to kill unwanted plants (weeds); insecticides to control pest insects; fungicides to control fungal diseases; fertilizers to provide nutrients; and diesel fuel to prepare the field, plant, and harvest the corn. These inputs are highly dependent on fossil-fuel energy. By contrast, an agricultural system designed on the model of nature's ecology will use biodiversity—over time and space—to circumvent the need for many of the inputs required in monoculture cropping systems.

A natural perennial ecosystem—such as Iowa's native prairie—tends to be much more resilient to extreme weather-related events than industrial monoculture cropping systems. For example, in 2008 eastern Iowa received heavy rainfalls which caused extensive flooding in late May and early June when the corn and soybean crops were very small or not yet planted. Because the soil was not protected by plant cover during the hard rains, soil erosion was extensive. Ten percent of Iowa's cropland lost 20 tons/acre of soil during that flooding event.[31] A dense perennial plant cover will not only do much better at protecting the soil from erosion during intense rainfall, but a perennial crop system will absorb more rainfall into the soil, reducing runoff and flooding severity. An Iowa State University study found that perennial crops absorbed five to seven times as much rainfall as corn and soybean crops during the first hour of a rainfall event.[32]

7

System Leakages Become Pollutants

A natural ecology does not cause pollution, because the waste of each species serves as food for other species of the ecosystem, serving as a built-in recycling system. Unlike the inherent recycling of waste materials by natural ecosystems, a characteristic of industrial agriculture is the tendency for leakages from the system to become pollutants to other systems. For example, the synthetic inputs (fertilizers and pesticides) of industrial corn production can become sources of pollution of surface and groundwater resources. When nitrogen and phosphorous fertilizers get into water resources, the result is eutrophication of lakes, elevated nitrate levels in drinking water and hypoxia in estuaries. An example is the hypoxia zone—often called the dead zone because aquatic life cannot survive in it—in the Gulf of Mexico at the mouth of the Mississippi River.

The Gulf hypoxic zone is caused to a great degree by leakage of nitrogen fertilizer through field tile drains and from there into rivers that drain into the Gulf.[33]

The nitrogen stimulates the growth of algae in a large area of the Gulf. The subsequent death and decomposition of the algae depletes the Gulf's water of oxygen. Fish, shrimp, and most other aquatic life cannot survive in water that is depleted of oxygen. One consequence of the annual hypoxic zone is economic hardship for family fishermen of the Gulf's $2.8 billion a year fishing industry.

Industrial livestock production also poses a threat to pollution of water resources. Large CAFOs produce large volumes of manure. One hog produces two to four times as much waste as an adult human. According to an EPA estimate, a farm with 2,500 dairy cattle will produce as much waste as a city of 411,000 people.[34]

The accumulation of such large volumes of manure makes CAFO systems vulnerable to spills during manure storage, handling, and applications to fields. Theoretically, CAFOs should not be a source of manure getting into water resources because CAFO owners are required by law to protect manure from spillage. They are required to develop and implement manure management plans that allocate all manure to fields at rates that do not exceed crop nutrient requirements. The problem is that state enforcement agencies universally lack the resources to oversee and enforce their rules for manure management to make sure that manure is stored and handled properly, and that it is applied in the places and at the rates specified in manure management plans. And even when applied at prescribed rates, manure applied to fields can be washed off during excessive rains and can leach down into field tile drainage systems and into surface waters.[35]

When manure gets into streams, rivers or lakes through leakage, spillage or over application, the waters' ecosystems can be greatly compromised. Nutrients from manure can cause algal blooms, and acutely toxic compounds in the manure—particularly ammonia—can kill aquatic life in the water body. According to the Environmental Integrity Project, records of the Iowa Department of Natural Resources document at least 329 manure spills resulting in the killing of more than 2.6 million fish over a 10-year period in Iowa.[36]

As will be described in more detail below, manure and other wastes generated in an ecological system are naturally spread diffusely over the landscape, where they are efficiently recycled by soil microorganisms right where deposited. When some wastes of a natural ecology do get into water resources, the diffuse distribution of those wastes means the impact is limited. A small amount of leakage of nutrients into surface waters is natural—and even desirable—in order to support food for aquatic life. However, concentrated nutrient inputs into surface waters can quickly overwhelm the ability of the aquatic ecosystem to absorb those nutrients, resulting in the death of aquatic species and a drastically altered aquatic ecosystem.

For example, the natural flow of nutrients down rivers to an ocean continental shelf contributes to a thriving fish population on the continental shelf. But when the nutrient flow down a river becomes excessive, algae growth will overwhelm the ecosystem at the mouth of the river, resulting in a hypoxia zone that will eliminate the fish population.

8

Agriculture and Climate Change

Climatologists tell us that our climate is changing. One of the causes of climate change is the growing concentration of heat-trapping "greenhouse gases" in the air. The most prevalent greenhouse gas (GHG) is carbon dioxide. However, in agriculture two other greenhouse gases are of major concern: methane, which has more than 20 times the GHG potency of carbon dioxide, and nitrous oxide, which has about 300 times the potency of carbon dioxide.[37] Agriculture contributes about 8 percent of total GHG emissions in the U.S.[38]

The release of nitrous oxide from soils is by far the largest source of GHG emissions from agriculture in the United States. Nitrous oxide emissions from soils can come from soil organic matter, legumes, manure, and other sources, but the largest source is from synthetic nitrogen fertilizer. About 2.5 percent of synthetic nitrogen fertilizer applied to crops can be released into the atmosphere as nitrous oxide.[39] If farmers were to diversify crop rotations by including more nitrogen-fixing crops in rotations, less synthetic nitrogen would be needed, reducing nitrous oxide emissions. That would also reduce the amount of fossil fuel required to synthesize nitrogen fertilizer, concomitantly reducing carbon dioxide emissions.

Methane is the second-largest source of GHG emissions from agriculture in the United States. More than 70 percent of agriculture's methane emissions come from enteric fermentation,[40] a fancy term for gas produced in the digestive tracts of animals, mostly cows and other ruminant animals. Because rumen fermentation is a natural process, enteric methane cannot be eliminated, although research is finding that adjusting feeding rations can help reduce enteric methane emissions.[41] [42]

In the United States, about a fourth of the methane from animal sources comes from manure after it leaves the animal. That source of methane can be greatly reduced with appropriate management. For example, when manure is deposited in pastures or is composted, very little methane is generated. However, when manure is stored in liquid pits, it becomes anaerobic (as will be explained below), creating ideal conditions for methane to be generated in the liquid manure pit.

Because hogs are not ruminants, they produce very little methane from enteric fermentation. Nearly 90 percent of methane emissions from hog production in the United States is generated from manure while it is stored in liquid pits.[43] Raising hogs on pasture or in deep-bedded housing would substantially reduce methane from hog production.

One "solution" that has been proposed to solve the

problem of methane emissions from stored liquid manure is to build methane digesters next to CAFOs to produce and capture methane from the manure. While it is true that methane digesters will reduce methane emissions and produce methane fuel, it is important to also consider some of the limitations of methane digesters. One limitation is that methane digesters require animals to be in confinement so that their manure can be collected to be put into the digester. Animals that are out grazing in pastures spread their manure on the landscape where the manure decomposes and returns the nutrients to the soil, and does not emit much methane during decomposition. Also, when animals are housed on deep-bedded manure packs that are composted, methane emissions are much less than when manure goes into liquid manure pits. In other words, methane digesters not only require an industrial-style livestock production system in order to operate, but also, they are only needed for prevention of methane emissions in an industrial-style livestock production system.

Also, methane digesters are very expensive to build and almost invariably require large subsidies to make building them feasible. While many types of energy systems are currently being subsidized, it should be noted that subsidies for CAFO methane digesters also indirectly serve as subsidies for industrial livestock production systems. CAFOs already often receive subsidies to build liquid manure storage systems. Subsidizing CAFO methane digesters will amount to a double subsidy for the growth of the industrial livestock industry.

When considering the benefits of methane digesters to reduce methane emissions from stored CAFO manure, it is important to consider that there are alternative livestock production systems—that will be discussed in more detail below—that circumvent the need for methane digesters because they do not use methane-emitting liquid manure storage systems.

Considered solely from the energy-production point of view, methane from manure is not a high-producing source of energy. That is because when animals eat feed they utilize most of the energy of the feed for their own metabolism, which means that their manure is much lower in energy than the plant materials they ate. For methane generators connected to CAFOs to produce a lot of energy, additional biomass will need to be added to the manure.

9

When Manure Is Not Manure

Sometimes, CAFO proponents attempt to downplay the insufferable odor of CAFO waste by saying "manure is manure." They argue that manure has been around for 10,000 years, so people who cannot tolerate being around CAFO manure should not live out in the countryside. That argument ignores the fact that liquid manure that is stored in a CAFO lagoon or pit undergoes radical transformation during storage, which completely alters its chemical nature and creates compounds that are not only foul-smelling but toxic.

The toxic compounds are created through a process of putrefaction caused by the lack of oxygen in the manure storage reservoir. Manure that is held in a CAFO's liquid storage reservoir begins to decompose, but because the liquid-manure environment lacks sufficient oxygen for complete decomposition, the system becomes anaerobic (without oxygen) and the manure putrefies. During the putrefaction of manure, more than 300 volatile organic compounds of varying degrees of toxicity are produced.[44]

Two of the more commonly known toxic compounds produced during liquid manure putrefaction are ammonia and hydrogen sulfide. Ammonia is an irritant that affects the eyes, nose, skin, and respiratory tract.[45] Long-term exposure to low levels of ammonia can lead to respiratory and pulmonary disease.[46]

Hydrogen sulfide, which has the characteristic smell of rotten eggs, is a neurotoxin. At high concentrations, hydrogen sulfide will cause rapid unconsciousness and death through respiratory paralysis and asphyxiation.[47] That is why when CAFO ventilation systems fail, the confined animals—and even CAFO workers—can quickly be overcome and die from hydrogen sulfide poisoning. Exposure to low levels of hydrogen sulfide has been associated with headaches, nausea, and respiratory infections.[48]

Other airborne emissions from CAFOs include odor, dust, allergens, and a wide variety of volatile organic compounds. Also, significant amounts of the greenhouse gases methane and nitrous oxide are created during liquid manure putrefaction.

The decomposition of animal manure under natural conditions is completely different from what happens to liquid manure in a CAFO. For example, when an animal deposits manure on the soil surface in a pasture, the manure lands on top of billions (literally) of soil organisms. The soil organisms quickly begin decomposing the manure. Unlike the anaerobic conditions in a CAFO liquid manure pit, the decomposition by soil organisms is an aerobic process; that is, it occurs in the presence of oxygen. When oxygen is present, the manure decomposes into carbon dioxide, water, and humus. Putrefied compounds are not produced. The aerobic decomposition of manure in a pasture is an odorless process.

Likewise, when manure is properly composted, it undergoes aerobic decomposition, and the finished compost is odorless and rich in humus-like compounds which, when used as a soil amendment, enrich the soil and sequester carbon. When hogs or other livestock are raised in deep-bedded hoop houses, the manure and bedding mixture they leave behind is normally composted, which is why properly managed hoop houses are not an odor problem.

Approximately 50 million tons of livestock manure are produced annually in Iowa.[49] With that amount of manure, it is easy to see that systemic problems in how manure is managed can produce a large degrading influence on water quality, air quality and the overall quality of life in rural areas.

10

Health Effects of CAFOs

Many studies from the 1970s through the 1990s found that workers in swine CAFOs suffer from a wide range of health problems, including respiratory problems such as chronic bronchitis, occupational asthma and organic dust toxic syndrome.[50]

Research in the 1990s found that neighbors of CA-FOs suffered from many of the same health problems found with CAFO workers. A Duke University study found that neighbors of CAFOs had significantly higher rates of tension, depression, anger, and fatigue than control groups.[51] A University of Iowa study found that neighbors of CAFOs suffered the same kinds of respiratory problems as CAFO workers.[52] A North Carolina study found that neighbors of CAFOs had significantly elevated rates of headaches, runny nose, sore throat, excessive coughing, diarrhea, and burning eyes.[53] In 1998, the Centers for Disease Control concluded that "adequate evidence currently exits to indicate airborne emissions from large-scale swine facilities constitute a public health problem."[54]

A 2006 study by the University of Iowa found that Iowa children attending school near a CAFO had a 24.6 percent asthma rate compared to 11.7 percent for children at a control school.[55] The study also found that children raised on hog farms had a 44.1 percent asthma rate, and that children raised on hog farms where antibiotics were routinely fed to hogs subtherapeutically had a 55.8 percent asthma rate.

A study published in the American Journal of Agricultural Economics in 2009 found that a doubling of CAFO numbers in a county was linked to a 7.3 percent increase in infant mortality.[56] In that study, an increase of 100,000 animal units in a county corresponded to 123 more infant deaths per year per 100,000 births.

In spite of these and other studies documenting the health effects of CAFOs, the CAFO industry continues to deny that toxic fumes from CAFOs are a health concern. The industry continues to fight any measures to control toxic gases emanating from CAFOs, claiming that the evidence of negative health effects is not yet conclusive enough. Their stance is reminiscent of the position of the tobacco industry years ago when evidence of the detrimental health effects of smoking was becoming very strong. A 1969 leaked memo of a tobacco industry executive said "Doubt is our product since it is the best means of competing with the 'body of fact' that exists in the mind of the general public."[57]

11

The Future of CAFO Agriculture

Earlier we observed that CAFO agriculture—the epitome of industrial livestock production—came into full development just as society in general began transitioning from the Industrial Age to the Information Age. We also observed that for agriculture, the Information Age means knowledge of ecology and how to design and manage crop and livestock systems in ways that are ecologically sound. CAFOs came into full development just on time to be obsolete. What will catalyze the transition from industrial livestock systems to livestock systems based on the economy of ecology? Three forces are already at work in manifesting that transition.

First, as consumers become more interested in where their food comes from and begin to make conscious choices of what they select to eat, they are beginning to demand food produced in alignment with their social and environmental values. When demand changes, agriculture responds to fill the new demand. Examples of this are the growing demand for—and production of—organic, free range, grass-based and locally produced food.

An example of agriculture responding to demands of consumers is the quiet 2009 disappearance of the use of rBST (recombinant bovine somatotropin), also known as bovine growth hormone, in the dairy industry. In response to consumer demands for milk from cows not treated with rBST, retail grocery chains informed dairy processors that they wanted dairy products produced without rBST. In turn, processors informed dairy co-operatives, and the co-ops informed dairy farmers that they would no longer accept milk from cows treated with rBST. It all happened rather quickly and quietly, without public announcements from the dairy industry that they were no longer using milk from cows treated with rBST.

Second, changes in laws and regulations at the state level are beginning to require changes in industrial livestock production methods. In a case that garnered national attention in 2008, Californians passed Proposition 2, which created a new state statute that will phase out the use of animal production systems that confine animals in small spaces in a manner that does not allow them to turn around freely, lie down, stand up and fully extend their limbs. The new California law takes effect in 2015. Michigan passed a similar measure in 2009 to become the seventh state to ban pig gestation crates, the fifth state to ban veal calf crates and the second state to ban battery cages for laying hens.

However, industrial livestock supporters have fought back. In a move to pre-empt similar laws from being enacted in Ohio, livestock industry leaders got a ballot measure before Ohio voters in November 2009 to amend the state constitution to create a livestock care standards board. Ohio voters handily passed the measure—which would stave off regulations like those of California and Michigan—by the same margin that Proposition 2 passed in California (63 percent of the vote). The 13-member Ohio board that the new law created would be comprised mostly of farmers, veterinarians, and agricultural industry leaders. The Board's charge was to create and implement livestock care guidelines.

Opponents of the Ohio measure argued that it was designed to ensure the continuation of business as usual in livestock production, and they mounted a counter initiative. They formed the group Ohioans for Humane Farms and gathered over half a million signatures for a new ballot initiative in 2010. In a compromise move, the Ohio governor brokered a deal between the Ohioans for Humane Farms and the Ohio Farm Bureau that would, over time, phase out the use of crates for veal calves and gestating hogs and would deny new permits for battery cages for laying hens.[58] Clearly, the regulation of confinement animal agriculture will be an ongoing issue across the country in coming years.

The third force that will push livestock production toward ecologically based systems is the escalating cost of energy. Industrial agriculture is predicated on cheap fossil fuel energy. An example below will illustrate how grass-based dairy production can take advantage of the efficiencies of ecosystem organization to circumvent much of the need for external energy inputs.

In 1998, I had the opportunity to visit Cuba on a scientific study tour with the Consortium for Sustainable Agriculture Research and Education. We saw firsthand how the Cubans had coped with the abrupt loss of petroleum-based fuel and pesticides when the Soviet Union collapsed and the U.S. embargo made it impossible for them to procure those inputs. Very quickly the Cubans transitioned from Soviet-style industrial animal production systems to grass-based systems. A few remnants of the previous industrial livestock era were visible around the countryside in confinement building structures that had been converted to housing for people and cattle feedbunks that had been converted to earthworm vermiculture containers.

Our tour guide in Cuba was Fernando Funes, Sr., a researcher at the Pasture and Forage Institute in Havana. Dr. Fernando showed us research they were conducting comparing the energy efficiency of several pasture-based animal systems. By their calculations, their former industrial livestock systems required about 10 units of energy expenditure to produce one unit of food energy. With the pasture systems they were studying, they had already achieved an energy efficiency of 10 units of food energy produced from each unit of energy expended—a 100-fold increase over their former industrial livestock systems—and their goal was to get at least 15 units of food energy from every unit of energy expended.

Dr. Fernando called the previous era of industrial animal production in Cuba "farming on wheels," in reference to the practice of that time to haul feed to the cows and haul the manure back to the fields.

Although the Cubans had an abrupt and difficult transition away from industrial agriculture—and even today are greatly handicapped by the embargo enforced against them by the United States—their experience with pasture-based livestock systems shows what is possible in a post-cheap-fossil-fuel era. Fortunately, in the United States, we still have time to prepare for the time when cheap fossil fuels will no longer be available. We should use that time to plan for, and begin the transition to, more energy-efficient animal production systems.

12

The Design of Nature's Ecology

Twelve thousand years ago, in the wake of the most recent glacier, the land that would become Northern Iowa was a geologic wasteland. Glacial materials conveyed from the north had obliterated the biological diversity of the previous era. But then nature's ecological processes began anew, creating—over 12 millennia—a prairie ecosystem with fertile, productive soils.

How did that happen? Gradually, plants, animals, and microorganisms colonized the desolate landscape, creating an increasingly diverse and complex ecosystem. The ecosystem's plants and animals generated organic materials which soil microorganisms consumed and used to develop fertile soils from raw geologic materials.

It has been estimated that 60 million bison once roamed the prairies and plains of North America.[59] (That compares with about 95 million cattle in the U.S. today.[60]) The bison traveled in large herds and their behavior contributed to the development of fertile soils in the areas they traveled. Bison herds roving the prairie landscape are a useful model we can employ to design animal production systems that are resilient, energy-efficient, biologically diverse and ecologically sound.

When bison herds grazed the tall, deep-rooted prairie plants, they reposited their manure nutrients back to the soil from whence the plant nutrients had come. And, their grazing activities stimulated regeneration and robustness of the ecosystem. After being grazed, the shortened prairie plants had excess root mass for their reduced above-ground leaf mass, so the plants sloughed a portion of their roots into the soil. As the plants grew new shoots and leaves above the ground, they also grew new roots below the ground. The root mass that had been released into the soil after the bison had grazed the prairie plants became food to sustain soil microorganisms and produce humus (sequestered soil carbon). Repeated grazing cycles of the roaming bison herds increasingly added to the soil's fertility, productivity, and organic matter.

As we will see, modern livestock production systems can be designed and managed to mimic the ecological processes that created the diverse prairie and its productive soils. And these systems can be much more energy-efficient than current industrial animal production methods. The key is to find ways to harness the energy, efficiency, and organizing power of nature's ecology. Modern scientific understanding of ecology provides insights into the design and management of these systems.

13

A Grass-Based Dairy Designed to Mimic Nature's Ecology

On the dairy farm that my wife, Susan, and I own and operate in southeastern Iowa, we base our farm's design and management on the principles of ecology. We moved our dairy from several miles away to its current location in 1996. The land we moved the dairy to had been under continuous corn and soybean cropping for many years previously, and the farm had no buildings we could use for the dairy. We had to design and build the dairy from the ground up.

The farmland had been cash rented from an absentee landlord before we bought it, and conservation had been neglected. The land on the farm is rolling and steep in places—with some hills exceeding 15 percent slope. Most of the field's grass waterways were gullied, with the deepest gully nearly four feet deep. Because the configuration of the landscape did not lend itself well to contour farming, convenience had dictated that row crops had been planted up and down some of the hillsides. In some areas of those hillsides, all of the topsoil was gone; that is, the surface soil—what soil scientists call the A horizon—had been lost to erosion.

We repaired the gullies and planted the cropland on the farm to a mixture of grazing forages, consisting of grasses and forbs, including legumes. Since all the buildings of the original farmstead had disappeared, (except an old wooden corn crib) we built new facilities, including a milking parlor, cattle barn, on-farm dairy processing plant and a house.

We divided about 120 acres of the new pasture into 60 small pastures—called paddocks—using simple, low-cost electric fencing materials. This paddock system allows us flexibility to manage where cows graze at all times, so we can optimize the productivity and nutritional value of the pasture forages. We manage the cows to mimic the ecological effects of bison herds roaming the prairie.

We milk about 80 cows twice a day on our farm. During the growing season, we turn the herd out to a new section of pasture after each milking. Normally, we give the milking herd half of a paddock—about one acre—to graze after each milking, twice every day. We can quickly and easily subdivide paddocks into any size increment using portable fencing materials.

Besides the milking herd, we have two other groups of grazing dairy cattle, each rotating through paddocks in separate areas of the farm. One other group consists of cows that are in the dry phase of their production cycle (each cow calves annually and for two months before calving is dried off—not milked) and pregnant heifers (heifers are young female cows). In the third group are the yearling heifers that are not yet old enough to be bred.

After a paddock has been grazed, we move the cows on to the next paddock, and the grazed forage in the paddock the cows had been in is allowed to rest and regrow as the cows rotate through other paddocks. In spring and early summer the grass grows fast, so we rotate the cows back to each paddock in about 20 or 30 days. As the summer gets hotter and drier, the forage growth rate slows, so we slow the rotation down to 40 days or more of recovery time before re-grazing a paddock. That allows the forage plants adequate time to recover and regrow from the previous grazing episode.

If they were not given adequate recovery time, the forage plants would become less productive over time, and eventually some plants would die from the stress of overgrazing. Good management promotes greater pasture productivity, higher nutritional value of pasture forages and greater diversity of forages—and ultimately more milk production per acre of land. Good pasture management also improves soil quality and fertility, helps protect water quality, and contributes to wildlife habitat. In short, we are rebuilding our farm's ecological capital, and improving the long-term productivity of the land.

We normally begin grazing the first week of April, just as the grass begins to grow vigorously. We start grazing early—even though the forage is then short—so that when we complete the first rotation cycle around the farm's paddocks, the forage in the paddocks that were grazed first has regrown to a prime stage for grazing again. That also sets the paddocks around the farm in a sequence of regrowth stages suitable to the timing of the paddock rotation cycle.

In early summer the pasture forage grows faster than the cows can graze it, so we harvest some of the paddocks as hay for winter feed. As the summer progresses and it gets hotter and drier, the forage growth slows, so we slow down the paddock rotation to allow more time for regrowth. Then, we bring those paddocks that had earlier been harvested for hay into the grazing rotation so it takes longer to move the cows through the full rotation of paddocks.

We are also able to continue grazing after the growing season ends in fall. To do that, we defer grazing some pasture areas in August and allow the forage there to grow and "stockpile" until the growing season ends in October. We then graze those areas throughout November and even into December, until the grass becomes covered by snow. By starting grazing as early as possible in the spring and stockpiling forage for grazing past the end of the growing season, we are able to lengthen the time the cows are able to graze each year to about eight months, and we reduce the amount of hay we need to harvest mechanically and store for winter feeding.

The grazing system that we use on our dairy farm mimics the prairiegrass/bison ecology that contributed to building the Midwest's deep, fertile prairie soils. However, unlike the roaming bison herds, we manage where our cows graze at all times, which allows us to optimize forage productivity and utilization and to maximize the rebuilding of soil "ecological capital."

Management is important. If paddocks are allowed too much recovery time, the plants will become overly mature and will lose nutritional value. With too little recovery time, some plant species will not recover fully and will die, reducing pasture productivity and diversity. Under good management, plant diversity is maintained or increased and soil fertility is continuously regenerated.

Over time, we have learned many simple management techniques that increase productivity and reduce energy needs. For example, we try to maintain our pasture forage mix at about half grass and half clover. Clover is an important component of the pasture forage mix because clover is a legume that fixes nitrogen from the air into a form the plant can use to make protein. (Nitrogen fixation by legumes is done through a symbiotic relationship between legume plants and rhizobia bacteria that inhabit the plants' roots. The symbiotic relationship allows the rhizobia to feed off plant roots for their energy needs while they convert inert nitrogen gas from the atmosphere into organic forms that the plants can use to make proteins.) With adequate clover in our pastures, we do not need to add any nitrogen fertilizer. For that matter, we do not add any fertilizers to our pastures beyond what is recycled back to the soil in the manure—which has been enough to not only replenish but to rebuild the soil fertility in the pastures.

Sometimes paddocks will become sod-bound as grasses begin to predominate and clovers fade from the pasture. To reverse that trend, we allow the cows to graze the sod-bound pastures during rainy times. That will allow the cows' hooves to cut through and open up the sod, allowing more spaces for clover plants to take root and grow. If clover plants begin to dominate over grass in some paddocks, we can allow those paddocks more rest time between grazing episodes, which will help strengthen the grass plants and increase grass presence in the paddock.

The design of a grass-based system is key to making it efficient to manage. We built rock-surfaced lanes throughout the pasture areas to allow the cows to walk from the milking parlor to all paddocks without making mud or causing soil erosion, and we have water tanks in all pastures so cows have access to water at all times. We use a solar-powered watering system for watering the cows in the pastures.

The solar-powered watering system is set up with an array of solar photovoltaic panels on the edge of a farm pond. The solar panels power a pump in the pond which pumps water to a 4,000-gallon tank located on top of the highest hill on the farm. The water then gravity flows from the large tank through an underground pipe system to all 60 paddocks on the farm, where there are small tanks for the cows to drink from. This water system saves us about $150 per month in costs we had previously paid for water from the rural water system (farmers in southern Iowa get most of their water from rural water systems because southern Iowa lacks abundant groundwater).

We are working on other renewable energy systems for our farm. In 2010, we installed solar hot water panels on the roof of our dairy processing plant to heat water for our processing plant and milking parlor. We are now making plans to install a wind turbine to produce electricity for the farm.

In 2010, we were able to purchase an additional 220 acres of land immediately adjacent to our dairy. Now, with about 450 total acres on the farm, we are looking to make our dairy as self-sufficient as possible for our approximately 160 head of dairy animals. We will be able to expand our operation incrementally as our market grows. We do feed some grain, currently about five to six pounds of grain per milking cow during the summer months when the cows are on pasture and 10 to 12 pounds of grain during the winter when the cows are on stored feed.

14

Value Added, Value Retained

The vast majority of dairy farms sell the milk they produce as milk raw in bulk to co-ops or companies that pick the milk up and take it to central processing facilities. We process our milk on the farm. Until a few years ago, we were the only dairy farm in Iowa that processed milk on the farm. By 2010, with growing consumer interest in locally produced food, there were at least six on-farm dairy processors in Iowa. On our farm we have a small dairy processing plant where we pasteurize our milk and produce bottled milk, yogurt, and several varieties of cheese. We market all our dairy products locally through grocery stores and restaurants within a five-mile radius of our farm.

Our dairy products have several features that add to their value to our customers: 1) our cows are Jerseys, which produce milk high in protein, butterfat, and other milk solids, giving them enhanced flavor; 2) our dairy products are grass-based, giving them unique nutritional features; 3) our dairy products are organic; 4) our dairy products are not homogenized; 5) our dairy products are produced locally.

By adding value to our milk on the farm and marketing the value-added products ourselves, we retain the added value to reinvest in our farm and increase its profitability. Our value-added, value-retained dairy also contributes to the local economy by providing jobs for six people (including Susan and me) for the local community. Also, since we sell our dairy products locally, the food dollars that local residents spend on our products circulate back into our community. If more small- to medium-sized farms were to produce value-added products on their farms, it would provide more employment opportunities in rural areas and help reverse the population decline of rural communities.

Value-added agriculture does not always equate with the added value being retained by farmers. For example, an ethanol plant adds value to corn. If the ethanol plant is owned by farmers, the value added is retained by the farmers. If the ethanol plant is owned by a multinational corporation based in another state, the value added is not retained by the farmers; nor is it retained in Iowa, beyond the jobs created by the ethanol plant.

15

Grass-Based vs. Confinement

Let's compare, for a moment, the energy efficiency of a grass-based dairy with a confinement dairy: When cows are kept in confinement, the cows' forage has to be mechanically harvested in the field, hauled to the confinement facility, placed in storage, and then mechanically removed from storage each day to feed the cows. And, the cows' manure must be collected into a storage facility from where it eventually must be hauled back to fields and spread. All these operations require fossil fuel energy.

By contrast, in a well designed grass-based dairy, the same objectives are accomplished by simply opening the gate to the next paddock. The cows walk to the paddock, harvest their own forage and at the same time spread their manure throughout the paddock in a way that is ecologically sound. And, they enjoy their work!

The irony of modern confinement animal production has been summed up by Allan Nation, editor of the Stockman Grass Farmer[61] in this way (paraphrased): It is the nature of cows to move about and the nature of grass to stand in one place, but with confinement animal production, we have turned it backward and made the cows stand in one place and made the grass move to the cows. Turning nature backward like that takes a lot of energy, and is only possible when energy is cheap. Now that we are at the end of the era of cheap energy, we will need to employ the organizing power of nature rather than fight against it.

Cows living and grazing in their natural environment are healthier than when living under confinement conditions, often on concrete. Also, a diet high in freshly grazed forage is healthier for cows than diets that are normally fed in confinement dairy systems. A cow has a rumen, which is a digestive system that evolved to digest forages. The rumen serves as a fermentation vat for bacteria that can digest the cellulose (which humans cannot digest) of forages. When a cow is fed high levels of corn or other grains—as is normal in CAFO dairies—milk production per cow is higher, but the cows are more susceptible to health problems, especially metabolic disorders and foot problems.

An additional benefit of grass-based dairies is that milk produced by grazing cows is higher in nutritional components found to be beneficial to human health,[62] including omega-three fatty acids, conjugated linoleic acids, beta carotene and some vitamins.

Our farm has now been under pasture-based perennial crop cover for 14 years. Soil erosion has been virtually eliminated, and soil productivity continues to improve.

Even the areas of soil where the A horizon had previously been eroded away are becoming productive and getting darker-colored from organic matter accumulation. In short, we are rebuilding the farm's ecological capital that had previously been lost through intensive row cropping..

Grass-based beef operations can be designed and managed in ways that are very similar to the dairy grazing system described above. If beef grazing operations do a very good job of managing pastures and maintaining highly nutritious forages, beef cattle can be finished—with high-quality meat—on forage, without having to go to a feedlot to be finished on corn. Hogs and poultry can also be raised on pastures. Management of hogs and poultry on pastures requires more intensive management than confinement systems, but substantially reduces the costs of housing and equipment.

Soil scientists tell us that in the approximately 150 years since Iowa's prairies were converted to crop production, about half of the topsoil has been lost or moved by erosion, and about half of the soil organic matter has been lost to oxidation. It was nature's ecology that created Iowa's deep, fertile soils—from a geologic wasteland left by receding glaciers many years ago. Therefore, it seems reasonable that if we can design and manage farming systems so they mimic the ecological processes that created our soils in the first place, we should be able to rebuild lost ecological capital and create truly sustainable farming systems.

16

Can Sustainable Farming Feed the World?

Proponents of industrial agriculture often proclaim that if sustainable or organic farming were widely adopted there would be mass starvation around the world. There are several flaws to that argument.

The first flaw is the assumption that converting to sustainable or organic farming means returning to the methods of 100 years ago. Clearly, that is not the case. While we can learn and apply many things from earlier traditional farming methods, advances in technology and increased understanding of biology and ecology have taken organic farming far beyond the farming methods of 100 years ago. Then, all farming was "conventional," because the distinction between organic and conventional had not yet been made. Since then, conventional and organic farming methods have diverged, and both have become much more productive.

Innovations in farm equipment over the years have benefited both organic and conventional farmers. For example, in the 1960's when my brother and I would cut hay using a tractor hitched to a converted horse mower on the farm we grew up on, it took the two of us about an hour to cut one or two acres. Today, on my organic farm, I can easily cut, condition, and windrow 10 acres of hay per hour by myself. In the 1960s, it took our family crew of four a long hard day to bale 50 tons of hay; today I can bale 50 tons in two hours, by myself. Also, today's organic farmers use mechanical weeders and guidance systems on cultivators to control weeds much more efficiently and precisely than possible in the 1960s.

But the greatest advancement for today's organic farmers has been an increased understanding of biology and ecology, and how to design and manage organic farms to efficiently utilize the energy and organizing power of nature's ecology. For example, as discussed earlier, new scientific understandings of grassland ecology help grass-based farmers better manage grazing in order to increase biodiversity and productivity and reduce the need for fossil-fuel-based inputs.

Also, new scientific advancements in understanding the ecology of insects, weeds, and plant diseases are helping organic farmers manage pests through the use of crop rotations, beneficial insects, pest mating disruptions and other cultural practices that circumvent the need for chemical pest controls.

Certainly, there is room for improvement in organic food production, just as there is in conventional production. However, it is remarkable that organic agriculture is as productive as it is today given the paucity of research funding for organic over the years. Long-term research comparing organic and conventional farming methods done by Iowa State University has found that corn and soybean yields of organic and conventional farming systems are similar.[63]

The agriculture research budget of the United States Department of Agriculture is approximately $2 billion annually. Before the 2002 Farm Bill—when $5 million was marked for organic research—there were virtually no USDA research funds specifically dedicated to research on organic agriculture. The 2008 Farm Bill raised funding for organic agriculture research to $15 million, a good increase but still meager in comparison to research funding for conventional agriculture. One can only wonder where organic agriculture production would be today if its research budget had been on par with that of conventional agriculture over the past 50 years.

A research team from Michigan compared yields of organic versus conventional agriculture by analyzing 293 existing data sets from around the world. They found that in developed countries, the yields of organic and conventional agriculture were about equal. But in developing countries, the organic yields were higher, often substantially so.[64] The study concluded "that organic methods could produce enough food on a global per capita basis to sustain the current human population, and potentially an even larger population, without increasing the agricultural land base."

A 2008 United Nations analysis of 144 projects in 24 African countries found that yields more than doubled where organic practices that maximized the use of on-farm resources were used.[65] In addition to yield increases, the study found that environmental benefits from organic farming in those studies included improved soil fertility, better retention of water and resistance to drought. The UN study concluded that "the evidence presented in this study supports the argument that organic agriculture can be more conducive to food security in Africa than most conventional production systems, and that it is more likely to be sustainable in the long term."

A key reason why researchers are looking to organic methods—particularly in developing nations around the world—is that organic methods optimize the use of locally available resources and biologically produced resources on site, rather than relying on expensive external inputs that are not readily available and are often too expensive for limited-resource farmers.

The Green Revolution of the latter 20th Century was a great triumph of increasing food production in food-deficit countries using the methods of industrial agriculture. However, scientists are now recognizing that some of the unintended consequences of the Green Revolution include extensive soil erosion, loss of soil fertility, loss of agricultural land through salinization, depletion of water tables, increased pest resistance and social disruption.

In 2008, the United Nations, World Bank and Global Environment Facility sponsored an International Assessment of Agricultural Knowledge, Science, and Technology for Development (IAASTD) by a team of more than 400 scientists and development experts from more than 80 countries.[66] The IAASTD team looked at policy options for how agricultural knowledge, science, and technology could reduce hunger and poverty, improve rural livelihoods and human health, and facilitate equitable and environmentally, socially, and economically sustainable development around the world. The team produced a comprehensive report in which they addressed the successes and shortcomings of past development efforts and made recommendations for future efforts. The report pointed out that past development efforts of the Green Revolution have produced large increases in food production, but those increases have come with significant environmental and social costs, and the challenge today "is to increase the productivity of agriculture in a sustainable manner."

The IAASTD team pointed out that "for many years, agricultural science focused on delivering component technologies to increase farm-level productivity," and argued that to increase food production in a sustainable manner requires recognition that agriculture is multifunctional. As the report framed it: "The concept of multifunctionality recognizes agriculture as a multi-output activity producing not only commodities (food, feed, fibers, agrofuels, medicinal products and ornamentals), but also non-commodity outputs such as environmental services, landscape amenities and cultural heritages."

The IAASTD report made recommendations for how agricultural knowledge, science, and technology could be applied in international development in ways that would "recognize and give increased importance to the multifunctionality of agriculture, accounting for the complexity of agricultural systems within diverse social and ecological contexts." The recommendations focused on eight areas in which the multifunctionality of agriculture should be considered:

- Bioenergy

- Biotechnology

- Climate change

- Human health

- Natural resource management

- Trade and markets

- Traditional and local knowledge and community-based innovation

- Women in agriculture

Applying the concept of the multifunctionality of agriculture would no doubt serve us well in the United States also. Often policies for agricultural production in this country run counter to environmental and social concerns. For example, U.S. crop subsidy programs in general provide the highest incentives for farmers to grow annual crops that can have the greatest potential harmful environmental effects, such as soil erosion and nitrate leaching to water resources. Another example is the existence of state-level laws that give higher priority to the economic returns of CAFO owners than to the health, quality of life and property values of their neighbors.

Some of the multifunctional aspects of agriculture that we in the United States should consider in our deliberations on agricultural policy include the viability of rural communities, the competitiveness of family farms, the health of farmers and rural residents, the resilience of farming systems to extreme weather events, the aesthetic and recreational value of the landscape, the nutritional value of the food we produce, the welfare of farm animals, the effects of farming practices on air and water quality, the compatibility of agriculture with wildlife habitat, and the long-term sustainability of our farming systems.

Designing agricultural policies that take into account the inescapable interconnectedness of agriculture's many roles will take more comprehensive thinking, but will provide ample payback in enhanced benefits for society and reduced externalized costs from agriculture. Such policies will move us beyond industrial agriculture to a multifunctional agriculture designed around nature's ecology, with long-term benefits for farmers and all of society.

Section II

Energy Solutions for Agriculture

17

Peak Oil Plateau

A major challenge on the doorstep of agriculture today is the escalating cost of energy, particularly oil. Iowa's agriculture is today highly dependent on oil-based inputs. When oil prices peaked at $147 a barrel in 2008, farm input costs went through the roof, putting agriculture in a perilous position. Diesel fuel and fertilizer costs tripled in price.[67] [68] The aftershocks of the 2008 oil price spike and fall were still being felt in 2010 in some segments of agriculture, particularly the ethanol industry.

In addition to the direct impact of higher energy costs, the instability of energy prices is particularly problematic for agriculture, especially with the amount of investments that have been made in recent years in the corn-ethanol industry. When oil prices rose rapidly in 2008, ethanol prices rose concomitantly, which in turn caused corn prices to soar. The sudden rise in corn prices not only caused financial hardship for the livestock sector of agriculture—with its reliance on corn—but it also ultimately came back to bite the ethanol industry when oil prices quickly dropped back down from $147 to under $40 per barrel. The ethanol industry suddenly found itself in the untenable position of having to pay high prices for corn—that it had forward-contracted at peak prices—while ethanol demand and prices fell. The whipsaw effect of rapidly changing energy and commodity prices caused more than a few ethanol plants to fall into bankruptcy.

Unfortunately, some oil economists are predicting that oil prices will continue on this roller coaster ride of highs and lows, with each cycle of price peaks and troughs being higher than the previous one. Economist Jeff Rubin makes a strong case for a roller coaster future for oil prices in his book "Why Your World is About to Get a Whole Lot Smaller."[69]

Using international data on oil reserves, production, and consumption, Rubin argues that we have hit a peak plateau in world oil production that will hold our oil-dependent world economy hostage in the future and will keep us in an unending series of boom-and-bust cycles, unless we are able to free ourselves from our oil dependency.

Rubin makes the case that the peak plateau in oil production will be the cause for back-to-back economic boom-and-bust cycles as follows: In today's international setting of rapidly expanding oil demand, when the world economy is booming and in an expansion mode, international oil production capacity cannot meet all needs. As a result, growing oil demand chases after an insufficient supply and oil prices spike sharply, as we saw in 2008. These high oil prices ripple throughout the economy. Some segments of the economy cannot operate with those very high oil prices and begin to shut down—industries close, transportation is reduced, etc. The ensuing economic recession and slowdown of industry results in a reduction in oil use. When oil use falls below the plateau in world oil production capacity, oil supplies suddenly exceed oil demand, causing oil prices to drop precipitously. When oil prices hit bottom, low-cost oil spurs industries to begin to ramp up again, helping the economy recover from recession. However, as the world economy gathers steam again, oil demand will rise again. Eventually, world oil demand will again pass oil production capacity, and oil prices will spike sharply once more. Rubin argues that not only will our economic future be a boom-and-bust roller coaster ride of this nature, but that oil price peaks and troughs will both get progressively higher each time, unless we are able to free ourselves from our oil dependency.

Rubin predicts that oil prices will hit $200 per barrel in the next price peak. That may seem high from today's perspective, but the $147 per barrel price peak of 2008 would have been considered absurdly high in 2007. In his book, Rubin, recounts a talk he gave to oil executives in Calgary's Petroleum Club in 2000. He told the oil executives that the alarmingly high price of oil they were experiencing in 2000 ($30 per barrel) was not a cyclic blip, but the beginning of the future trend in oil prices. He told them to expect $50 per barrel oil within

five years. His oil price forecast was met with amuse-
ment and derision by the oil executives, who were
themselves thinking that world oil production would
soon be increasing and would bring oil prices back
down to $20. By 2005, the price of oil hit $50 per barrel.

In 2005, Rubin was invited back to the same venue to
give a forecast update on the outlook for oil prices. He
predicted that oil prices would double in the next two
years, to $100 per barrel. Again his prediction was met
with disbelief. Oil broke through the $100-per-barrel
ceiling in January 2008.

Rubin's argument that we have reached a peak plateau
in world oil production is based on data indicating that
oil fields around the world are being depleted as fast as
new oil fields are coming on line. Four million barrels
per day of new oil production capacity must come on
line every year to replace what is being lost through depletion. Of course, more than that is required if we add
in the need to meet the rapidly growing demand for oil
in developing countries like China, India, Brazil, and
others. Moreover, Rubin points out that oil-exporting
countries—like Saudi Arabia, Russia, Venezuela, Iran,
and other Middle East countries—are increasingly
cannibalizing their own oil supplies through their
growing domestic consumption, reducing the amount
available for export into the world market.

Although there are still a lot of known untapped world
oil reserves, they are not being exploited faster than the
rate of oilfield depletion and growing world demand,

according to data cited by Rubin. As a result, world oil production capacity is at a plateau. He argues that the reason new oilfields are not being developed faster is because most untapped reserves will be harder and more expensive to recover, and the volatility and uncertainty of oil prices is making oil investors nervous and hesitant to make large investments in oilfield development. For example, it costs $90—and 1400 cubic feet of natural gas—to recover one barrel of oil from the Canadian tar sands. Until oil price troughs rise to near $90, the tar sands will be slow to develop.

Rubin is not alone in his analysis. Lester Brown, president of Earth Policy Institute, cites evidence that Mexico, China, and Saudi Arabia have peaked in oil production and are entering a period of production decline.[70] In addition to the four million barrels per day of new oil production capacity that must come on line every year to replace what is being lost through oilfield depletion around the world, Brown estimates it will take an additional 2 million barrels per day to meet growing world demand. Brown cites Sada al-Husseini, former head of exploration and production at Aramco, the Saudi national oil company, as saying that to fill that shortfall will require the production capacity of "a whole new Saudi Arabia every couple of years. It's not sustainable."

Even the U.S. military is concerned about the prospects for world oil production to keep pace with demand. In a 2010 report of the United States Joint Forces Command, military planners project that "by 2012, surplus oil production capacity could entirely disappear, and as early as 2015, the shortfall in output could reach nearly 10 MBD" (million barrels per day)."[71]

18

Energy Use in Agriculture

Agriculture today is highly dependent on fossil-fuel energy. Even a causal observation of today's industrial agriculture leads to the inescapable conclusion that our system of agriculture would not be possible without cheap fossil fuels. We use fossil fuels to power our farm machinery, manufacture fertilizers and pesticides, dry crops, transport crops and livestock, and produce our electricity.

However, agriculture has become more efficient in its energy use in recent decades. Total energy use by agriculture dropped about 29 percent between the late 1970s and 2004.[72] Much of that increased energy efficiency came from conversion of farm machinery from gasoline to diesel fuel, and from reduced fuel use through reduced tillage practices.

Even with increased energy efficiency over the last three decades, agriculture is still highly dependent on fossil fuels, particularly oil. When oil peaked at $147 per barrel in 2008, diesel fuel hit nearly $5 per gallon, and some fertilizers peaked at $1,200 per ton. If the next oil price peak hits $200, diesel will be near $7 per gallon and fertilizer more than $1,600 per ton, if their price increases are proportional to what happened last time. Using the same proportional price increases, when oil spikes to $300 per barrel in the future, diesel will go to nearly $10 per gallon and fertilizer will spike at $2,400 per ton. One has to wonder what the breakpoint is for our industrial agricultural systems to become priced out of the oil market.

These projected high prices for farm inputs are alarming in themselves, but are much more alarming in the context of extreme price volatility. If farm input costs were to increase gradually over time, it certainly would put a burden on farmers to pay increasingly higher prices, but it also would allow time for markets to adjust by building those increased costs into higher prices for products leaving the farm gate. However, when input costs fluctuate wildly over short time frames, all segments of agriculture become imperiled. For example, if oil prices spike and set off a spike in fuel and fertilizer prices just when they are needed for the next year's crop, farmers will not only be strapped with high costs to get their crops in the ground, but they will also be in the precarious position of not knowing if and when crop prices might rise enough to cover the high planting costs, or if crop prices might crash by harvest time.

This effect of market volatility will ripple through all sectors of agriculture, and will be particularly destabilizing when the rising and falling prices of inputs and outputs are mismatched. When farm costs of inputs like fertilizers fall quickly, input suppliers can get caught with a stock of inventory that they paid high prices for which no one now wants to buy because prices have fallen and farmers can get it cheaper elsewhere. The corn-ethanol industry can get caught with contracts to buy corn at high prices when corn has fallen to much lower prices on the open market—and when ethanol prices have plummeted along with oil prices—putting them in the untenable position that their cost to produce ethanol exceeds the market price of ethanol.

19

Biofuels: Cars vs. Agriculture

Clearly, the way out of being held hostage by high oil prices is to become a lot less dependent on oil. While there may be many strategies agriculture can pursue to reduce dependency on oil and other fossil fuels, they generally fall under two major categories: 1) become more energy-efficient in order to reduce energy needs, and 2) replace fossil fuels with renewable energy sources. First, let's explore alternatives to fossil fuels. Then, as we will see, some of the energy alternatives come with built-in efficiencies that will reduce the total energy needs of agriculture. Furthermore, the alternatives we will look at can make our farming systems more resilient, environmentally sound and sustainable.

Can biofuels be used to power agriculture? Already today some biodiesel is being used as an energy source for agriculture, but the predominate biofuel produced today is ethanol, which is used to power passenger vehicles driving down highways. In other words, agriculture is producing cheap raw material (corn) for the production of biofuel (ethanol) for off-farm use, while paying high retail prices for fossil fuels to power agriculture. That arrangement not only puts agriculture on a path to a perilous future when fossil fuels become excessively high-priced or in short supply, it also puts farmers on the short end of the "economic stick" in both transactions. As President John F. Kennedy said: "The farmer is the only businessman in our economy who has to buy everything at retail, sell everything at wholesale and pay the freight both ways." We can do better than that with energy for agriculture.

In 2009, we burned through 139.5 billion gallons of gas—including 10.6 billion gallons of ethanol—to power passenger vehicles in the Unites States.[73] To make those 10.6 billion gallons of ethanol, we used about 30 percent of the U.S. corn crop. Could we use that capacity for biofuels production more wisely and efficiently? Could we convert that biofuels production capacity into systems to power agriculture? To try to answer those questions, let's first look at how efficiently we use ethanol in the United States today.

To start, let's do a couple of simple calculations: The 10.6 billion gallons of ethanol that we used in 2009 equals about 7.6 percent of the 139.5 billion gallons of gas burned by passenger vehicles. If we account for the fact that ethanol yields only two-thirds as much energy per gallon as gasoline, the ethanol displaced just 5.1 percent of our gasoline. If we were to consider transforming our current biofuels production capacity into systems to power agriculture instead of automobiles, how much would we need to increase our automobile gasoline mileage by to replace the ethanol lost from transportation?

According to EPA estimates, the average passenger vehicle mileage (including SUVs) for 2008 model vehicles is 20.8 miles per gallon (mpg).[74] If we were to increase that mileage efficiency by 5.1 percent (to replace the lost ethanol), we would need to bump our mileage up by just 1.1 mpg, to 21.9 mpg. In other words, a 1.1 mpg average increase in passenger vehicle mileage would save as many gallons of fuel as all the ethanol produced today, which requires 30 percent of our U.S. corn crop to produce.

How difficult would it be to increase our average mileage by 1.1 mpg? Clearly, we have the technology today to increase mileage many times more than that. For example, for the past five years, I have been driving a gas-electric hybrid vehicle (which seats four to five passengers) that gets about 44 miles per gallon—more than double the average mileage of passenger vehicles in the United States today. Furthermore, plug-in hybrid technology that is available today could quadruple the current average mileage. That means that we have the technology available today to save 10 to 30 times more fossil oil through increased automobile efficiency than what we save by burning ethanol.

If we would double our automobile mileage, we would reduce our annual gasoline usage from 140 billion gallons to 70 billion gallons. That 70 billion-gallon savings would dwarf the 11 billion gallons of ethanol we produce in the United States today. Clearly, increasing fuel efficiency is a more effective and environmentally sound way to reduce fossil oil use than replacing gasoline with corn ethanol, particularly given the external environmental costs of producing corn ethanol. Even if we continued to add 10 percent ethanol to gasoline as an oxygenate, if we reduced our gasoline use by 70 billion gallons per year, we would reduce our ethanol needs by 7 billion gallons per year. That would free up 15 million acres of land that are now producing those 7 billion gallons of corn ethanol for automobiles. Those 15 million acres of land could be used to produce biofuels to power agriculture, as will be described below.

Some of the more common reasons given for producing ethanol for automobiles are 1) to reduce our dependence on foreign oil, 2) to reduce smog and greenhouse gas emissions, and 3) to provide economic development. Through a combined approach of rapidly increasing our passenger vehicle mileage and converting our biofuels industry to systems that power agriculture, we could make much more progress on all three of those fronts. Not only would we reduce oil consumption—and greenhouse gas emissions—by automobiles through the improved mileage efficiency, we would also reduce fossil oil consumption on farms if we converted our biofuels production capacity to making biofuels for farm use. That would reduce farm fuel costs, reduce automobile fuel costs, and drastically reduce imports of foreign oil and emissions of greenhouse gases. It would be a win-win-win result.

20

Limits of Using Contemporary Energy

When we talk about the end of cheap oil and converting agriculture—and society in general—to renewable energy sources, it is important to recognize some fundamental differences between fossil fuels and renewable energy. First, as the name implies, fossil fuels were formed hundreds of millions of years ago from plant life, which derived its energy from photosynthesis using ancient sunlight over millions of years. In other words, fossil fuels are concentrated ancient solar energy that accrued over a long time.

Most contemporary renewable energy systems are also powered by the sun. Biomass, photovoltaic, solar thermal, wind, hydropower, and even ocean wave power derive their energy from the sun. A big difference between using the ancient solar power of fossil fuels and using contemporary solar power is that, with the latter, our energy budget is limited to the daily flux of energy from the sun. In reality, it is further limited by our capability to capture and utilize solar power on an ongoing basis. With fossil fuels, the only limitation is how fast we can extract and process them—until they become depleted. In fact, we will never completely extract the world reserves of fossil fuels because the reserves become increasingly difficult to extract as they get closer to depletion, until we reach the point at which it takes more energy to extract the fossil fuels than the energy they contain.

When we are constrained to using contemporary solar power, our energy budget will no longer be seemingly unlimited, as with fossil fuels. That means that we will need to look for large gains in energy efficiency. It is unrealistic to expect that our energy-dependent system of industrial agriculture will remain unchanged at the end of the cheap-oil era. We will no doubt be required to make fundamental system changes in agriculture—and in society—to be able to thrive on contemporary solar energy. An important consideration for making the transition to renewable energy is to begin the transition before nonrenewable energy costs become so high that agriculture becomes priced out of the market. To fail to do so will be to invite chaos and likely fuel—and even food—shortages.

21

Toward Sustainable Energy Self-Sufficiency for Agriculture

A three-pronged approach for moving agriculture toward sustainable energy self-sufficiency is 1) convert to farming systems with lower energy requirements, 2) develop systems to produce renewable energy on farms that can be used to power farms and 3) convert to more resilient cropping systems—like perennial crops—for biofuels production. Fortunately, for biofuels production, the three approaches can be complementary to each other.

It would be unrealistic to think that if we just convert to biofuels to power agriculture our industrial agricultural systems can carry on as usual. There is no silver bullet to securing agriculture's energy future, no one thing—like biofuels—that will do the job. Borrowing a metaphor from Bill McKibben,[75] what we will need is "silver buckshot"; that is, we need to develop a variety of approaches that all together can keep agriculture productive and profitable. And, the agriculture of tomorrow will surely look different from the agriculture of today.

Now, most ethanol is made from corn grain. Efforts have been ongoing for years to develop the technology for a next generation of ethanol production using cellulosic feedstocks. This technology has not developed as rapidly as originally anticipated. In 2007, Congress enacted the Energy Independence and Security Act, which mandated the use of 36 billion gallons of ethanol by 2022, of which 21 billion gallons is required to be from cellulosic ethanol and other advanced biofuels (derived from feedstocks other than corn starch).[76] The technology for achieving efficient ethanol fermentation from cellulosic plant material is not developing quickly enough to meet the schedule of that mandate.

Aside from the technical difficulties of making ethanol from cellulose, there are other reasons to question if large-scale cellulosic ethanol production is the best direction for future biofuels development. The relevant questions are related to the sheer scale required for centralized production of cellulosic ethanol. Compared to corn grain, cellulosic plant feedstocks are only about one fourth to one fifteenth as dense, depending on how compacted they are, which means that much more volume of cellulosic plant material would have to be hauled to an ethanol plant to produce as much ethanol as an equivalent weight of corn grain. Hauling that much cellulosic plant material to ethanol plants would be a transportation challenge, and would add considerable cost to cellulosic ethanol production. Also, to handle so much biomass volume, a cellulosic ethanol plant would need to be much larger than a corn-grain plant to produce an equivalent amount of ethanol, which means that the capital costs to build a cellulosic ethanol plant will be significantly higher.

On the positive side, an advantage of using cellulosic feedstocks for biofuel production is that perennial crops could be used as feedstocks. However, when we talk about using perennial crops for biofuels, we are not referring to just ethanol production. As we will see below, there are other biofuel systems that look promising.

Many perennial crops could potentially be used for biofuel feedstocks, including prairie plants like switchgrass, or mixed polycultures of prairie plants. One promising crop for cellulosic biomass production is miscanthus, a tall-growing perennial crop that can produce 12 to 20 tons of biomass per acre, two to four times the yield of switchgrass.[77]

There are several advantages to using perennial crops instead of annuals for biofuels production. First, perennials cover the soil year around, helping protect the soil from both erosion and nutrient loss to water resources. Annual crops, like corn and soybeans, actively grow for only about five months out of the year. That leaves the soil vulnerable to erosion and nutrient loss during the other seven months of the year.

For every gallon of ethanol produced from corn, about two gallons of soil are lost to erosion, based on the soil erosion rate for cropland in Iowa (5.7 tons/acre) published in the USDA National Resource Inventory,[78] and the five-year corn yield average for Iowa (173 bushels/

acre) from the USDA-National Statistical Service.[79] Erosion rates for soils under perennial crops is one-half to one ton/acre, about a fifth to a tenth of that under annual cropping systems.[80]

Nitrate leaching is also reduced dramatically under perennial crops. Research at the University of Minnesota compared the amount of nitrate leached out of the soil profile through field tile drains during four years of a corn/soybeans rotation in comparison to four years under continuous perennial plant cover.[81] In the corn/soybean rotation, 181 pounds of nitrate-nitrogen/acre was leached into field tile drains and from there into surface waters during the four years. In the same study, under a perennial alfalfa field, just six pounds/acre of nitrate-nitrogen leached, and under perennial grass enrolled in the Conservation Reserve Program, only four pounds/acre leached into tile drains. Clearly, perennial crops are more protective of soil and water resources.

There are other efficiencies to be gained from replacing annual crops with perennials for biofuels production. Perennial crops for biomass would require much less—or no—herbicides, insecticides or fungicides compared to what is normally used for corn production. And, because perennials do not need to be replanted each year, the fuel required for preparing a seedbed and planting corn each year would be avoided. Moreover, the fertilizer needs for perennial crops for biomass would be much less than for corn.

Research has found that at the end of the growing season, perennial plants translocate a high percentage of their nutrients—especially nitrogen—from the aboveground portion of the plant back down to the roots as the plant goes into dormancy in the fall.[82] That means that if the biomass harvest of the perennial crops were delayed until after the plant went dormant in the fall, most of the nutrients would be preserved below the soil surface, and little or no additional fertilizer would be required the following spring. Studies have shown that because of the greatly reduced need for fossil-fuel-based inputs of perennial crops over annuals, perennial crops could potentially produce much more net energy per acre than corn.

According to the Iowa Renewable Fuels Association, "corn ethanol production generates 67 percent more energy than it takes to produce."[83] By comparison, a Midwestern study estimated that switchgrass grown for biofuel production would produce 540 percent more energy than it takes to produce it.[84] And, miscanthus could potentially provide more than twice the net energy of switchgrass.[85]

22

Pyrolysis

Pyrolysis is a term which, though hard to spell, will soon be a household word. Pyrolysis is a process of heating biomass in the absence of oxygen to produce combustible fuel and a byproduct called "biochar." Biochar is a charcoal-like substance that has many uses. A primary use for biochar, that we will discuss later, is as a soil amendment that increases soil fertility while very effectively sequestering carbon in the soil.

How does pyrolysis work? To understand pyrolysis, it is helpful to first understand the normal process of combustion of a fuel. Combustion requires three things: fuel, heat, and oxygen (usually, the oxygen comes from the air). When a solid fuel such as biomass is burned, heat first causes the solid material to begin to vaporize. The gases produced are ignitable, and if oxygen is present the gases will burn. However, if a solid fuel—like biomass—is heated in the absence of oxygen, the biomass will vaporize but the combustible gases produced will not ignite because there is no oxygen present to allow the chemical reaction of combustion to occur. Therefore, the combustible gases can be captured and stored, or transformed into other types of fuels. In other words, during pyrolysis, the process of combustion is initiated but not allowed to proceed to the point of burning the fuel.

Pyrolysis is not new. During World War II, when petrol fuel was short, many European cars were converted to being powered by pyrolysis, using wood as the fuel source.[86] Although it is probably not practical to consider pyrolysis for powering automobiles on a large scale today, it does demonstrate the potential to use pyrolysis for fuel production on a scale much smaller than the large ethanol plants we normally think of when we talk about biofuel production. Pyrolysis may be a key technology for producing renewable energy at a farm scale. Any plant material—or for that matter, any organic material—including prairie grasses, wood, and landfill wastes can be used as a fuel source for pyrolysis. And pyrolysis will provide as much or more energy per unit of biomass than fermentation of the same biomass into ethanol.[87]

When the gases produced by pyrolysis are cooled to room temperature, the heavier gases (larger molecules) condense to liquids, which are called bio-oil. The lighter gases, like hydrogen and methane, which remain gases at room temperature, are called "syngas" (synthesis gas).

By changing the conditions (temperature and speed of heating) of pyrolysis, it is possible to optimize for one or more of the three products of pyrolysis (syngas, bio-oil and biochar). For example, slow pyrolysis under lower temperatures will produce more biochar whereas fast pyrolysis at higher temperatures will produce more bio-oil. With fast pyrolysis, the syngas that is produced can be burned within the system to maintain the temperature, resulting in bio-oil and biochar as the products of pyrolysis.

Bio-oil is a low-grade oil that has properties similar to No. 2 diesel fuel. However, bio-oil is higher in oxygen and water, is more corrosive, and tends to vary somewhat in its makeup depending on the biomass source used.[88] Bio-oil can be used directly in a furnace adapted for its use, or can be blended and used in diesel engines. Bio-oil can also be fermented to produce ethanol.

Bio-oil can also be further processed into "green diesel" and "green gasoline," which can be used in place of their petro-based counterparts.[89] This has tremendous potential application for producing fuel for farm use, and perhaps even for producing fuel at the farm level.

One advantage of cellulosic pyrolysis over cellulosic ethanol production is that pyrolysis may be more easily adapted to smaller-scale production facilities. With small-scale units, many pyrolytic production units could be distributed throughout the countryside, resulting in shorter hauling distances for the voluminous cellulosic feedstocks used for biofuel production. Smaller scale equipment would also mean lower cost to set up individual pyrolytic units, which would make them more affordable for local ownership, either by farmer co-operatives, or custom operators, or even by individual farmers. One company in Canada has developed mobile pyrolytic production equipment[90] that could easily be pulled from farm to farm with a pickup truck, not unlike mobile seed-cleaning equipment that can travel from farm to farm to clean seeds.

With small-scale, distributed pyrolysis production of bio-oil, the transportation costs for hauling bio-oil to central processing for further refinement would be less than what would be required to haul the large volume of cellulosic biomass to central processing facilities. Ideally, the goal should be to develop technology to produce green diesel and gasoline on a farm scale using pyrolysis.

23

Biochar

As mentioned above, one of the products of pyrolysis is biochar, a charcoal-like substance. In fast pyrolysis, which optimizes for bio-oil production, biochar comprises 12 to 15 percent of the end product.[91] In slow pyrolysis, the biochar yield can be 50 percent or more.[92]

Biochar has many potential uses. It can be burned as a fuel, and it has many potential commercial and industrial uses. But, probably the most important potential use for biochar is as a soil amendment. When added to soils, biochar increases the water-holding and nutrient-holding capacity of soils, thereby reducing the need for irrigation and fertilizers. Biochar has a very long residence time—hundreds or even thousands of years—in soils before being degraded. That makes biochar an ideal soil amendment for long-term carbon sequestration. In other words, biochar additions to soils could make an important contribution to carbon sequestration to reduce the amount of greenhouse gases in the atmosphere.

The Amazon Basin contains areas of deep, rich, dark

soils which local people call *terra preta* (black earth). Those black earth soils are known to have almost magical qualities of rejuvenation and nearly inexhaustible fertility.[93] The soil in that area of Brazil is otherwise thin, red, and infertile. For many years, the origin of the *terra preta* soils befuddled archeologists and anthropologists. Only in the late 20th Century was the idea of the human origin of those soils accepted. It is now widely believed that *terra preta* soils were created by an indigenous population between 450 BC and AD 950 by amending the soils with a charcoal substance created by a form of pyrolysis. The resiliency and productivity of *terra preta* soils indicate that adding biochar from pyrolysis to soils today could contribute greatly to soil fertility and food production as well as sequester large amounts of carbon into soils.

The world's soils contain about twice as much carbon as is in the atmosphere.[94] That means that the soil has a very large capacity to serve as a carbon sink to help mitigate climate change. However, carbon can also be lost from soils when they are farmed. Much of the organic carbon of virgin soils was lost when they were put under crop production. For example, Midwestern prairie soils have lost about half of their original carbon in 150 years of crop production.[95] Biochar additions to those soils could not only rebuild soil organic matter levels by sequestering carbon but also increase soil productivity.

It is exciting to think about the many potential benefits of pyrolysis, particularly if the technology can be developed to produce green diesel and gasoline on a farm scale:

1) It would allow farmers to produce fuel on the farm to power the farm, allowing farmers to reduce or eliminate fossil fuel purchases.

2) For farmers who produced more fuel than needed on the farm, it would provide a higher-value product to sell compared to raw materials like corn or other biomass.

3) Regular biochar additions to soils would increase soil organic carbon, improving soil productivity and drought tolerance, and reducing irrigation and fertilizer costs.

4) Soil biochar additions would sequester carbon, reducing agriculture's carbon footprint and helping mitigate climate change.

5) Emissions of the greenhouse gases methane and nitrous oxide from soils are reduced when biochar is added to soils.[96]

6) Perennial crops could be used as the biomass source for pyrolysis, helping to protect the soil from erosion and nutrient loss, and reducing the amount of fossil-fuel-inputs—such as fuel, fertilizers, and pesticides—needed to grow annual crops.

7) Yard wastes and many household, commercial, and industrial organic wastes could be diverted from landfills to transformation into fuel and biochar through py-

rolysis, reducing waste streams to landfills, and methane (a potent greenhouse gas) production in landfills.

24

Sorghum for Ethanol

There are a number of alternative biomass sources that are being explored for biofuels production. One example that may have potential is growing algae and converting the algal biomass to biofuels. That could work particularly well in combination with an electric power plant that can serve as a source of both heat and carbon dioxide to spur algal growth.[97] Another interesting idea that is already being put into practice by an Iowa farmer is on-farm ethanol production using sweet sorghum.

Lee McClune, a Knoxville, Iowa farmer, grows sweet sorghum, from which he produces "sorghanol" (ethanol from sorghum).[98] He has developed harvesting equipment that enables him to press the juice out of the sorghum plants right out in the field. He then transfers the juice to a bladder to which he adds bioagents to aid fermentation. The sorghum juice is ideal for making ethanol because of its high sugar content, and fermentation takes only a few days. Once fermented, the solution is stable and can remain in a sealed container for months before distillation. The fermented solution, which is about 10 percent ethanol, could be sent to a central processing center for distillation. However, McClune is building his own distillation unit that will allow him to produce ethanol on the farm. McClune estimates that he can get an ethanol yield of 800 gallons per acre from sweet sorghum. To match that ethanol yield with corn—at a yield of 2.8 gallons of ethanol per bushel of corn—would require a whopping 286 bushels per acre of corn yield.

Although sweet sorghum is an annual crop, and so lacks some of the energy and environmental efficiencies of perennial crops, it has some advantages over corn. Sorghum is more drought-resistant and has lower fertilizer needs than corn. Sorghum is also planted later in the year than corn, which means that if a cover crop like rye or vetch were planted in the fall before the sorghum cropping year, the cover crop would have more time to grow and produce biomass (and the vetch legume would biologically fix more nitrogen in the soil) before the cover crop had to be killed in preparation for planting the sorghum.

Research at The Land Institute indicates that it may be possible to perennialize sorghum.[99] That would make sorghum an even more attractive crop for biofuel production.

A key difference between growing corn to deliver to an ethanol plant and doing something like producing ethanol on the farm with sweet sorghum, as Lee McClune does, is that McClune is producing a value-added product on his farm. And, very importantly, the value added on his farm is value retained on his farm. When value is added to commodity crops by a distant processing facility owned by an out-of-state company, that value added is lost to the farm, to the farmer's rural community, and even to the farmer's state.

25

On-Farm Wind Power

In recent years, the amount of electricity generated by wind power in wind-rich parts of the country has grown rapidly. Twenty percent of the electricity generated in Iowa now comes from wind power.[100] Most of Iowa's wind-generated electricity comes from large wind farms in northwest and north central Iowa where the state's wind resources are strongest. However, three-quarters of Iowa's land surface has wind speeds high enough to be favorable for installation of wind turbines.[101] That means that Iowa still has a large untapped potential to harness wind power. What has been largely overlooked is the potential benefit of farm-scale wind turbine systems.

There are several potential benefits of having small to medium-sized wind turbines on farms all across the state. First, that would allow more distributed production of electricity across the state. With distributed production, electricity generation within the state would be more constant because as wind systems move across the state, they will power turbines from one end of the state to the other, rather than just hitting regional clumps of wind farms and then passing by.

A second benefit of distributed production is that more of the electricity generated is used locally, either on the farm where it is produced or close by. That reduces the line loss that occurs when electricity is transmitted a long distance, and it reduces the need for high capacity transmission lines that become necessary when electricity from large wind farms in one area of the state has to be distributed across the remainder of the state.

An obvious benefit of having farm-scale wind turbines on farms is that those turbines power the farms they are installed on, and excess power generated serves as a farm income source. When power companies build and own wind farms on farmers' land, the farmers receive an annual lease payment, but the farmers must continue to pay retail rates for the electricity they use to power their farms.

Wind is a natural resource, much like oil or mineral reserves underground, except that unlike oil and mineral reserves, wind is an inexhaustible natural resource. If a landowner had an oil field underground, he or she would not likely lease it to an oil driller for pennies on the dollar, as landowners do with wind farm developers. When wind farms are owned by out-of-state companies, the profits—and sometimes even the electricity generated by the wind—are exported out of the state. Profits from wind power generated on farms—by turbines owned by farmers—will benefit farmers, local communities and the state economy.

Conflicts between wind farm owners and landowners

living next door to large turbines have been increasing recently as more large wind farms are built. That type of conflict is largely avoided where smaller-scale turbines are installed on land owned by the same person who owns the turbine.

Years ago in much of the Midwest, nearly every farm had a windmill on the farmstead to pump water from the farm well. Those windmills are mostly gone now, but they demonstrated that harnessing wind power can be an integral part of a farmstead operation. A farm-scale wind turbine placed strategically on a farmstead would need only a small footprint, and would probably not require an additional access road.

How can we make it affordable to install wind turbines on farms all across the state? The Europeans have already designed a good policy model for that: feed-in tariffs. Feed-in tariff (FIT) policies are used in more than 40 countries and are considered to be the primary reason for the rapid growth of the German and Spanish renewable energy markets.[102] A number of U.S. states are now considering FIT policies to speed up the adoption of renewable energy systems.

A FIT policy can be designed in a number of ways, but in general it requires a utility company to purchase electricity from eligible renewable-energy sources (for example, targeted wind and solar systems) at an increased price for a guaranteed period of time (typically 15 to 20 years). To spur the rapid adoption of farm-scale wind turbines across the state, a FIT policy could be implemented that would allow a landowner to install a wind turbine on her land and receive a payment rate per kilowatt hour that would equal the payment installments of the loan the landowner had on the wind turbine. At the end of the time specified by the FIT policy, the turbine would be paid for and the rate the landowner received per kilowatt hour would drop down to wholesale rates.

The obvious benefit of an FIT program to a landowner is that the landowner could have a wind turbine up and running with little or no cost. A down payment could be offset with tax credits. Or down payments might be unnecessary with the use of guaranteed loans. When the FIT time period ends and the turbine is paid for, the turbine will still provide electricity for the farm and serve as a farm profit center.

The costs of building farm-scale wind turbines under an FIT program like the one described above would be covered by all electricity users, just as the costs of building new coal-fired or nuclear power plants are. The benefits of this type of FIT program to a power company are: 1) after the FIT time period expires, the power company will get "green" energy at low cost for the lifetime of the wind turbines; and 2) during the years of the FIT period, as electricity costs rise (as expected) the FIT rate will increasingly become a better deal for the power companies.

Another policy option for making renewable energy systems accessible and affordable for farmers and homeowners is a Property-Assessed Clean Energy (PACE) program. Under a PACE program, local governments can establish a bonding program to finance renewable energy and energy efficiency projects for businesses and homes. Individuals can then borrow money from the bond fund and repay the loan through a special assessment on property taxes over a long period (typically 20 years).

The state's economy would also receive a boost from the investment and jobs created for manufacturing, installing, and maintaining the many farm-scale wind turbines. Feed-in tariff policies could also be used for other renewable energy systems, such as solar photovoltaic electricity generation.

26

Creative Uses of Wind Power

The National Renewable Energy Laboratory has estimated that Iowa has the technical potential to increase
its wind power development by over 150 fold.[103] Of
course, that full potential is not practically achievable,
given constraints on land uses, but clearly, that is an
indication that we have a lot more wind power potential than what we need for electricity generation. What
other technologies are on the horizon that might allow
us to use wind power to replace fossil fuel energy?

One potential use for wind-generated electricity is
to power electric and plug-in gas/electric hybrid cars.
Electric and hybrid cars can be charged at night, when
electrical demands are lowest and wind-power gener-
ating capacity might otherwise go unused.

If we were to develop a "smart" power gird, electric cars
could serve as a storage medium for wind-powered
electricity, as is already being experimented with in
Denmark. Here is how it works: If a commuter has an
electric car that can go 100 miles on a charge, and her
commute to work is ten miles one way, she can charge

her car at home overnight during off-peak hours, drive to work in the morning, plug her car into a meter connected to the electrical grid and sell 70 miles worth of electricity back to the grid during the hours of peak electrical demand. She can drive home in the evening with 10 miles worth of power to spare.

In an experiment with this kind of smart grid technology, the island of Bornholm, Denmark is hoping to increase its percent of electricity powered by wind from 20 to 50 percent.[104]

Technology is also in development that will allow rapid recharging of electric vehicles.[105] With technology for rapid recharging of batteries, or rapid battery exchange, electric refueling stations for highway vehicles could become an additional service of gas stations. And, in suitable areas, a wind farm of turbines on the refueling station site—backed up with batteries or some other storage medium—could provide much of the power for electric vehicle recharging. Another possibility for powering rapid-charge refueling stations would be for them to have a small electrical power plant on site that was fueled with biomass from perennial crops—like miscanthus—that were grown nearby the refueling station.

The University of Minnesota West Central Research and Outreach Center (WCROC) is working on some exciting technologies for use of wind power. Researchers there are using a wind turbine to make hydrogen by electrolysis.[106] Hydrogen can be used to power internal combustion engines and fuel cells, both of which could have applications for powering farm equipment.

The WCROC is also going a step farther and converting the hydrogen produced by wind power into anhydrous ammonia, which is a widely used form of nitrogen fertilizer. The WCROC project leaders estimate that the current demand for anhydrous ammonia fertilizer in Minnesota could be met with a little more than 2 gigawatts of wind power. They point out that if Minnesota could generate its anhydrous ammonia fertilizer through wind power, the state would retain the $300 million that now leaves the state to pay for its imported anhydrous ammonia. They estimate that anhydrous ammonia could be produced by wind power in the Midwest at a lower cost than the nitrogen fertilizer that is now shipped in from the Gulf of Mexico and Canada.[107]

The Hydrogen Engine Center[108] in Algona, Iowa has developed technology to adapt internal combustion engines to run on either hydrogen or anhydrous ammonia. That points to another exciting possibility for utilizing wind power. If we can make anhydrous ammonia with wind power, and we can power internal combustion engines with anhydrous ammonia, we have the potential to power agriculture with fuel derived from wind power. Unlike hydrogen, anhydrous ammonia can be easily stored as a liquid, which means that tractors and transport vehicles (even automobiles) could carry an amount of anhydrous ammonia fuel equivalent to the diesel or gasoline carried by current vehicles.

This technology points to the possibility that wind turbines owned by local farmer cooperatives—or maybe even by individual farmers—could make anhydrous ammonia locally, which could be used as a fuel to power farms, or could be used for nitrogen fertilizer. Also, if highway vehicles were adapted to run on anhydrous ammonia, the potential exists to build wind farms that produce anhydrous ammonia on the sites of highway refueling stations so the fuel could be made on site.

Compressed air is another possible medium for storing the energy of wind-generated power. Wind turbines could be made to power air compressors directly, or they can generate electricity, and that electricity could be used to power air compressors to compress air into storage systems. Engines that run on compressed air have been in existence for two centuries[109]

An advantage of compressed-air as a medium to store wind power on farms is that wind power could be used to power farm equipment when the wind is not blowing. The compressed air could be used to directly power machinery that run on compressed air, or the stored compressed air could be used to run an electrical generator that would provide the farm's electrical needs when the wind is not blowing.

Prototype automobiles have been built that are powered by compressed air and can travel up to 120 miles on a tank full of compressed air.[110] Hybrid compressed air/gasoline vehicles could go much further. Automobiles with engines that run on compressed air can have their storage tanks refilled about as quickly as a gasoline-powered car's fuel tank can be refueled. Like with anhydrous ammonia, compressed-air refueling stations could have backyard wind farms to create reserves of compressed air for automobile fill-ups. Vehicles powered by compressed air, or hydrogen, or anhydrous ammonia, or electricity would have zero carbon emissions if their fuel source were created by wind power.

Although many exciting possibilities can be envisioned with today's emerging technologies, it is important to keep in mind that the scenarios described above depend on contemporary energy—that is, from energy generated by the sun today. Unlike fossil fuels, the capture of contemporary energy—harnessed from today's sunlight—cannot be accelerated by speeding up extraction and processing, as can be done with oil wells and refineries, and with coal mines and coal-fired power plants. Being restricted to using contemporary energy will require us to become much more efficient in our energy use. In transportation, that will likely mean conversion to mass transit systems wherever possible, and use of highly efficient automobiles where mass transit is not feasible. In agriculture, that will mean conversion to animal production systems that allow the animals to harvest most of their own feed. It will also mean converting to perennial cropping systems as much as possible, because of their reduced energy requirements, and in general seeking energy efficiencies in all farming operations.

27

Imagine

In my youth, it would have taken a vivid imagination to think that in 40 years I would be carrying around a personal communication device that would allow me to instantly communicate with anyone around the world, and to have instant access to the latest information and cutting-edge knowledge of every field of life—at the touch of a few buttons.

Likewise, today we probably cannot fully envision what the future portends. However, we should not limit our thinking to a projection of the status quo of today, and we should not naysay about technologies on the horizon because they are not yet fully developed. Sometimes people who say things cannot be done need to get out of the way of people who are already doing them. As Abraham Lincoln purportedly said, "The best way to predict your future is to create it."

Let's try to envision a prosperous and sustainable Iowa farm in the post-cheap-oil era. Three principles the farm's design will need to accommodate are 1) resiliency, 2) energy efficiency and 3) energy self-sufficiency.

Resiliency means the farm can withstand the growing extremes of weather events due to climate change without the farm's ecological capital being compromised. A resilient farm would probably have mostly perennial crops on the landscape. Where annual crops are grown, cover crops would be used to protect the soil during fall, winter, and spring.

Energy efficiency would be gained through the use of perennial crops because of their lower energy requirements for tillage, fertilizers, and pesticides. The farm would be designed so that animals on the farm, particularly ruminants, could efficiently harvest most of their own feed. Perhaps advances in developing perennial grain crops, as is being worked on at the Land Institute in Kansas,[111] would allow harvest of grains from perennial crops.

The farm's energy requirements would be greatly reduced because of its energy efficiency. Energy needs would be met by a variety of energy sources. Solar hot water panels could provide hot water for the home and farmstead, and could also be used to heat the home and other farm buildings. Solar photovoltaic panels could be used to power a variety of farm systems, such as electric fence chargers, pumps for watering livestock and electricity for the homestead. As photovoltaic technology improves and becomes more cost-effective, it could become a primary source of electrical power for very efficient farmsteads. A wind turbine on the farm would complement solar power; often when the sun is not shining the wind is blowing. Some kind of storage mechanism for wind power described above could be used for when neither the sun was shining nor the wind blowing, and for during times of peak power use.

A portion of the farm's land could be devoted to raising crops to be harvested as biomass for making liquid fuels to be used in mobile machinery like tractors, trucks, and cars. The biomass crops would be perennials, such as woodlands or perennial grasses and legumes, and would be turned into fuels on the farm. If pyrolysis were used to convert biomass to fuel, the biochar by-product would be returned to the soil, increasing the soil's fertility and productivity and sequestering carbon in the soil.

Some people fear that when cheap oil runs out we will be forced to turn the clock back a century and live like our great-grandparents did. That could be the case if we do not plan for the end of cheap oil and suddenly find ourselves without. But if we plan for the future and use the remaining oil (not so cheap anymore) to transition our agriculture—and society in general— to a new era of energy efficiency and truly renewable energy systems, we may be able to create a future that is even more prosperous and fulfilling than today. In short, we need to create a future we desire, not be forced into a future created by the default of our own shortsightedness.

28

Energy Policy

A scientist friend of mine recently said to me privately, "corn ethanol is not part of an energy policy, it is part of a corn policy." He also pointed out that corn ethanol is not really a renewable fuel because both corn production and ethanol production are highly dependent upon nonrenewable fossil fuels. He makes some good points. It could also be argued that the crops most heavily subsidized by federal farm programs provide the least resilience on the landscape and are the least resource-conserving. For example, the most heavily subsidized crops in Iowa are the annual crops corn and soybeans which, as we saw above, create the most vulnerability for soil erosion and nutrient loss to water resources.

It is very difficult to achieve rational agriculture and energy policies today because every special interest group lobbies hard for policies that advance its own interests. Auto makers and oil companies oppose higher automobile mileage requirements; crop commodity groups lobby for subsidies for their own commodities; corn growers and ethanol companies lobby for subsidies for corn ethanol; and livestock commodity groups lobby against subsidies for corn ethanol because a lot of corn going to ethanol means high corn prices for livestock production.

In 2007, Congress got stirred into a fervor for ethanol and passed the Energy Independence and Security Act (EISA), which requires the production of 36 billion gallons of biofuels a year by 2022. It may be considered sacrilegious for a farmer to even ask the question, but is that good environmental—or even economic—policy? An analysis by Rice University's Baker Institute for Public Policy reported that in 2008, the U.S. government spent $4 billion in biofuels subsidies to replace about 2 percent of the U.S gasoline supply, at a cost to taxpayers of $1.95 per gallon of ethanol, on top of the price they paid for the ethanol at the pump.[112] The Baker Institute report concluded that Congress should revisit the mandates of the EISA.

If Congress could conjure up as much enthusiasm for mandating increased automobile fuel mileage as they have for subsidizing corn ethanol, we could make some real progress in reducing our dependence on foreign oil.

Many states spent a lot of money on subsidies and tax credits to build ethanol plants during the ethanol rush of 2007 and 2008, in spite of forward-thinking economists cautioning that the ethanol industry was overbuilding to an unsustainable level. When the price of oil plummeted in 2009, and took the price of ethanol down with it, ethanol plants went through an economic meat grinder. Many of them reduced production or shut down; some went bankrupt. Now that the price of oil is on the rise again, and is bringing ethanol prices up with it, there is a danger that we may find ourselves in a second wave ethanol rush, especially if EPA approves of raising the ethanol/gasoline blend rate from 10 to 15 percent.

It is high time to rethink biofuels policies on both federal and state levels. However, we now have a lot of taxpayer money invested in creating the ethanol infrastructure that is present today, and the farm economy and production have become geared to the ethanol industry. We can't change policy abruptly and jerk the rug out from under the ethanol industry. What we can do is first decide what the best long-term energy strategy is for the 21st Century, and then formulate policies that can take us there as quickly as possible without defaulting on commitments to the current biofuels infrastructure.

A good place to start with energy policy is to end state subsidies and tax credits for building new corn ethanol plants. That will avert another ethanol rush the next time oil prices spike. Those state resources saved from subsidizing more ethanol plants should be redirected toward developing emerging biofuel technologies that can power agriculture, and that use perennial crops for feedstocks, and that can be adapted to farm-scale production so the value created by biofuel production is retained on the farm. State feed-in-tariff policies for locally owned wind and solar electrical generation should also be a high priority, as should tax credits for farm-scale biofuel systems once that technology is fully developed.

On the federal level, Congress should revisit the EISA biofuels mandates and allow the Environmental Protection Agency or the Department of Energy to tweak the mandates annually to ensure that the existing ethanol industry remains viable without creating pressure for its further expansion. Congress should also gradually reduce, and eventually eliminate, the ethanol blenders subsidy and the ethanol import tariff as the ethanol industry becomes able to stand on its own economically. The federal government should also increase its commitment to research and technology development of energy systems for agriculture that are truly renewable, environmentally sound and profitable for farmers.

Section III

Local and Regional Food Systems

29

Where Does Your Food Come From?

Food is so familiar and intimate to our daily experience that most of us rarely think about where it comes from. We don't stop to think that the apple we are eating may have come from China, or the tomato from Mexico, or the grapes from Chile. We just know that they all come from the grocery store.

Farmers sometimes deride consumers for taking food for granted, for not knowing where their food comes from and assuming it will always be there. However, as Neil Hamilton, law professor at Drake University, has pointed out, most farmers don't really know where the crops they grow go to either. For the most part, farmers sell their production into commodity markets. The corn a farmer sells to the local grain elevator could end up feeding animals on his neighbor's farm, or it could be shipped all the way to China.

Perhaps that is just fine—we don't need to know where our food comes from or goes to as long as it keeps on coming and going. On the other hand, there may be reasons why we would want to know where the food we eat comes from. Some of those reasons could include freshness, taste, nutritional value, economics, food safety and food security.

In the United States we have never faced widespread food shortages. We have to use our imagination to comprehend that a billion people on our planet suffer from hunger or starvation. In our culture of abundant food, it can be a big challenge for us to not become part of the statistic of 1 billion people on the planet who are obese or overweight.

Yet, in the midst of the food abundance in our country, 49 million Americans suffer from hunger.[113] Even Iowa, the so-called "Food Capital of the World,"[114] ranks 26th in the United States in the prevalence of hunger (food insecurity), with 11.6 percent of Iowa's citizens lacking access to enough food to fully meet their basic needs at all times due to lack of financial resources.[115]

Certainly we could produce a lot more of the food we eat locally. We have done so in the past. In 1920, there were 34 crop and livestock commodities produced for sale on at least 1 percent of Iowa farms.[116] That number steadily declined over the years to less than 10 today. Fruits and vegetables were prominent on the list of commodities in 1920 but had completely fallen off the list by 1978.[117]

As part of the WWII war effort, the U.S. government rationed food and called on citizens to plant "Victory Gardens" to grow their own fruits and vegetables.

Twenty million Americans planted Victory Gardens in back yards, empty lots and even on rooftops. It was estimated that Victory Gardens provided up to 40 percent of the nation's food supply.[118]

First Lady Eleanor Roosevelt planted a Victory Garden on the White House lawn to inspire Americans to become more food self-sufficient during WWII. Today, First Lady Michel Obama has again planted a garden on the White House lawn, this time to inspire Americans to eat a healthier and local diet. The timing is right; consumers are increasingly seeking out locally produced food as part of their regular eating experience, for a variety of reasons. Let's explore some of the reasons why you might want to eat food produced near you.

30

Because It Tastes Better

Imagine a tomato picked green in Mexico, boxed up and shipped to Iowa. By the time it gets to the grocery store shelf, it begins to turn pink and even a little red. Now, imagine picking a red, vine-ripened tomato in your back yard. You can practically "taste" the difference in your imagination.

Beyond its superior flavor, produce ripened on the plant can be nutritionally superior.[119] For example, the Vitamin C content of tomatoes will increase to some degree after picking, but it will not reach levels found in tomatoes allowed to vine ripen.[120] Also, local fruits and vegetables generally get to consumers more promptly after harvest and at the peak of freshness, which contributes to retaining their nutritional value.[121]

There are several other reasons why locally produced food might taste better and be nutritionally superior. Most varieties of fruits and vegetables sold in national and international markets were selected primarily for yield and the capability to withstand long-distance transport. Selecting varieties for these genetic traits can come at the expense of compromising taste or nutritional quality.[122] Farmers producing food for local markets are more likely to prioritize taste and nutritional quality over durability and yield when choosing varieties of fruits and vegetables to grow.[123]

Food produced for local markets is generally harvested within 24 hours of delivery. Fruits and vegetables packaged and shipped long distance can undergo a number of post-harvest stresses that can compromise quality. Bruising during transportation, and mechanical harvesting of mass-produced fruit and vegetables, can reduce nutritional value.[124]

Harvested fruits and vegetables continue to respire and remain enzymatically active after harvest, causing them to suffer changes in nutritional value and loss of texture and flavor during storage and transport, especially if the temperature, atmosphere, humidity, and sanitation are not well regulated.[125]

There is evidence that when growers use production methods that improve the soil, such as the use of compost and cover crops, the resulting crops are higher in nutrient content.[126] Of course, there is no guarantee that local producers will use these soil-building methods, but many do. When buying from local producers you can query the producer about the farming methods used, including whether or not pesticides were used on the food you are buying.

31

Economic Development

Iowans eat $8 billion worth of food annually, but about 90 percent of that food is imported from out of state[127]—another ironic statistic from the "Food Capital of the World." Growing more of our food right here in Iowa represents a potential multi-billion dollar economic development opportunity. This potential economic activity could create thousands of new jobs and help revitalize rural communities in Iowa, as well as provide Iowans with fresh, nutritious food. It would also increase the biodiversity on Iowa's landscape.

Iowa State University researcher Dave Swenson has estimated that if Iowans ate the recommended five servings of fruits and vegetables per day, and Iowa farmers produced that food for just three months of the year, the production and marketing of those additional crops would add $302.4 million and 4, 095 jobs to Iowa's economy.[128] And it would not displace very much commodity corn and soybean production.

How much land would have to come out of corn and soybean production to produce the fruits and vegetables eaten in the Midwest? Relatively little. In another study, Swenson estimated that it would take the land equivalent of only about one Iowa county to produce 25 to 50 percent of 28 fruits and vegetables eaten in six Midwestern states. The farm-level income generated from that fruit and vegetable production would be $882 million, with a retail value of $3.31 billion. [129]

Swenson's study concluded that for every job displaced from corn and soybean production in Iowa, an estimated five jobs would be created for fruit and vegetable production on the same amount of land. That means that growing more of our food locally equals more jobs and increased rural economic development.

How large does a "farm" need to be to be profitable? An advantage of growing food for local consumers is that it can take a lot less up-front capital to get started than for large-scale commodity production. One system for getting started in intensive vegetable production, called SPIN (Small Plot INtensive) Farming,[130] provides guidelines on how it is possible to gross more than $50,000 on half an acre of land. This scale of farming can be done on vacant lots in urban areas. Of course, intensive vegetable production requires a lot of physical work—and certainly won't pay the salary of a Wall Street broker. However, commodity agriculture has not been so lucrative in recent times either.

Studies by Ken Meter of the Crossroads Resource Center have indicated that commodity agriculture production has generally been unprofitable or only marginally profitable in recent years.[131] Using data from USDA and the U.S. Bureau of Economic Analysis, Meter compared the income from agricultural commodities with the costs of producing those commodities. Meter did the analysis for various regions around the country and found that in many cases the net income was negative.

For example, in an eight-county region of northeast Iowa, farmers sold an average of $1.08 billion worth of crop and livestock commodities per year during 1999–2003. Yet they spent $1.14 billion to raise those commodities. The result was an average loss of $62 million in production costs for the region each year.[132] That loss was offset by an average of $173 million of federal subsidies, and $72 million of other farm-related income (primarily custom work and rental income) each year. During the same timeframe, consumers in the eight-county region spent $400 million per year buying food imported from outside the region.

The net result of commodity agriculture production and consumer food purchases in that eight-county region was a large drain of wealth from the region. Of the $1.14 billion spent to raise agricultural commodities each year, $500 million was spent buying supplies from outside of the eight-county region. That $500 million, combined with the $62 million loss from commodity production (calculated above) and the $400 million sent out of the region to buy food, equals a $962 million loss of potential wealth from the region's food and agricultural system each year.

Meter has found similar results in other regions of the United States, indicating not only that commodity agricultural production can be a net drain on a region's economy, but that importing food from outside the region further exacerbates the drain of the region's financial resources. Meter's analysis provides a sobering look at the value of our commodity food and agriculture system to local economies. It also points to the conclusion that producing food locally is a way to retain food dollars locally, making real contributions to local economies.

32

Healthy Foods Make Healthy People

In 1960, we in America spent 5.2 percent of our Gross Domestic Product (GDP) on health care.[133] By 2008, our health care expenditures had more than tripled, rising to 16.2 percent of our GDP. On the other hand, our food costs over the same time period followed the opposite trend, falling from 17.5 percent of our disposable income in 1960 to 9.6 percent in 2008.[134]

Obviously, many factors have influenced the costs of food and health care over the years, but those statistics lead to the inescapable question of whether the dwindling cost of our food is somehow related to our escalating costs for health care. The U.S. Centers for Disease Control (CDC) estimates that 75 percent of U.S. health-care costs are for chronic diseases that are linked to diet.[135] The health-care cost for diabetes alone is $116 billion annually,[136] and, the link between diet and Type 2 diabetes is well established.[137] Our shift away from healthy foods, like fruits and vegetables, and toward foods high in sugar, fat, and salt are no doubt a factor.

For example, high consumption of sugary soft drinks is linked to diabetes, heart disease and obesity.[138] [139]

Obesity in the United States now costs $147 billion annually in direct medical costs, according to Thomas Frieden, Director of the CDC.[140] Among the CDC's recommendations for combating obesity are recommendations for eating healthier foods, including the recommendation that communities and local governments "should provide incentives for the production, distribution, and procurement of foods from local farms."[141]

In recent years, there have been a number of nationwide outbreaks of food-borne illnesses from microbiologically contaminated food. The nature of our global industrial food system, with comingling of food from many sources and distribution over a wide area, increases the potential for isolated incidences of food contamination to be spread to much larger volumes of food and to afflict a large number of people. And, when food travels thousands of miles and changes hands multiple times, there are more opportunities for contamination. Local food production is generally smaller scale, less processed and not comingled with other foods, so isolated instances of food contamination are contained rather than becoming widespread.

The average food item travels 1,500 miles to get to your dinner plate.[142] That may need to change in the future as rising energy costs cause transportation costs to soar. In his book *Why Your World Is About To Get A Whole Lot Smaller*,[143] Jeff Rubin argues that rising oil prices will soon require us to look locally for goods and services—including our source for food. As oil prices escalate, the lamb chops from New Zealand and winter grapes from Chile may go the way of the Hummer.

33

Connecting Farmers and Consumers

The opportunities for consumers to buy food directly from farmers have been increasing. In Iowa, there are now 223 farmers markets, and farmers market sales have increased 92 percent over the past five years.[144] Farmers markets give consumers the opportunity to meet the farmer who produces the food they eat and to ask questions about how their food is produced.

Another system for farmers to market directly to consumers is Community Supported Agriculture (CSA). A CSA is a community of consumers who essentially pledge to support a farm operation for the duration of a growing season. CSA members become like shareholders and share in the risks and benefits of the farm's food production for the season. Members pay for the season in advance to cover the costs of the farm operation and the farmer's salary. The advantages of CSAs for farmers are that they can do their marketing during the off season; they receive payment early, which helps with the farm's cash flow; and they can get to know the people who eat the food they grow. The advantages for consumers are that they get to know their farmer and can ask questions about how their food is grown; they get very fresh food; and they get to visit their farm and learn more about farming and new foods. According to the USDA, in 2007 there were 12,549 CSAs in the United States.[145]

There are a number of other direct marketing opportunities for farmers. Farmers with U-Pick farms grow crops that are harvested by customers who come to the farm. That relieves farmers of much of the burden of harvesting and gives customers the opportunity to experience a farm and reduce the cost of their food. Roadside stands and farmstead marketing can also be good options for farms located near a well traveled highway, allowing them to get near-retail prices without having to deliver to a distant market.

A growing number of farmers market directly to restaurants. Restaurants will even sometimes put the farm name and products on the menu if a farmer can provide a consistent high-quality product. Selling directly to schools and other institutions is another growing opportunity for farmers. A number of state, federal, and privately supported programs are now available to help farmers connect with school lunchrooms, college dining halls, hospitals, and other institutions. These connections not only support local farmers, but also improve the nutritional quality of institutional food and can provide health and nutrition education for students.

The Internet can be used as a direct marketing tool for

farmers. For example, the Iowa Food Cooperative uses online marketing to connect farmers and customers. Farmer members can upload information on product availability and prices on the co-op's website.[146] Customers browse the site and put the food items they select into their virtual shopping carts. The farmers deliver the ordered food items to a central drop-off point once a week where their customers stop to pick them up. Because the co-op lists products from many farmers, customers have a wider choice of food products available than is generally possible through a CSA. And unlike a CSA, customers know exactly what they are getting. An advantage of this system to farmers is that, unlike a farmers market, they know exactly what is sold before they deliver, so they don't have to bring home unsold product.

Another opportunity for farmers is for them to work together and partner with other segments of the food chain to create regional food systems. A regional food system can be thought of as consisting of a value chain of many links. The sequence of links can be delineated as:

1) input supplier
2) farmer
3) processor
4) distributor
5) wholesaler
6) retailer
7) consumer

The Leopold Center for Sustainable Agriculture has done some work in helping farmers form value chain partnerships so they can get better market access for their products.[147]

In the northern climate zones of the continental United States, the length of the growing season is a major limiting factor for local food production. A short growing season not only limits the amount of production possible but also can make it difficult for farmers to develop long-term relationships with restaurants, grocery stores and institutions that require a year-around food supply. It usually takes a food purchaser who is sold on the benefits of local food and local economies to make local food purchases work in coordination with ongoing food purchases from national suppliers.

To increase their ability to produce local food for longer during the year, farmers can lengthen their growing season with greenhouses or low-cost structures like high tunnels, which can extend the growing season by as much as 10 weeks.[148]

34

Food Policy

The U.S. Department of Agriculture has formally recognized the economic and many other benefits of local food production in a new program called "Know Your Farmer, Know Your Food," which is encouraging the expansion of local food production across the country. When rolling out the new program, Secretary of Agriculture Tom Vilsack pointed out that creating new markets for local food will create wealth in rural communities. He said, "An American people that is more engaged with their food supply will create new income opportunities for American agriculture."[149] He added, "Reconnecting consumers and institutions with local producers will stimulate economies in rural communities, improve access to healthy, nutritious food for our families, and decrease the amount of resources to transport our food."

Secretary Vilsack pointed out that there is a growing number of small farms in the U.S., many of which grow food for their local communities. "In the last five years, we saw 108,000 new farming operations get started with sales of less than $10,000," Vilsack said. "These are very small farms, but they are a very important component of our agriculture." In Iowa, during the same five-year period, we saw an increase of 4,000 new small farms.[150] The growing number of new small farms in Iowa—juxtaposed with a report from Iowa's Leopold Center for Sustainable Agriculture that there are 64 grassroots organizations in Iowa working on expanding local food production and consumption[151]—bodes well for the potential to expand local food production in Iowa.

The state of Illinois passed legislation in 2009 to encourage more local food production in that state. The Illinois Local Food, Farms, and Jobs Act set procurement goals of local farm and food products for purchases of food funded by the state. One goal of the legislation is that by 2020, 20 percent of all food and food products purchased by state agencies and state-owned facilities will be produced in Illinois. State-owned facilities include prisons and public universities.

A second goal of the legislation is that by 2020, 10 percent of all food and food products purchased by entities that are at least partially funded by state dollars will be produced in Illinois. This category includes public schools, child care facilities and hospitals.

The Illinois legislation also created a Local Food Council that will help facilitate meeting these goals. Illinois' legislation seems like a reasonable approach that other states like Iowa could well emulate. We could probably think of many more policy options to increase local food production, if we decided to make that a priority for the state.

A policy option proposed by Robert Marqusee, Director of the Woodbury County (Iowa) Department of Rural Economic Development, is to allow grocers a 20 percent tax credit on all food purchased through contracts with local farmers.[152] Marqusee points out that 94 percent of all food purchased through grocers is presently produced outside of Iowa, which means that most of the food dollars spent at grocery stores leave the state. Using a conservative $1.38 multiplier for every dollar spent locally, Marqusee argues that his proposed tax credit would deliver a net financial benefit to Iowa's economy by retaining and recirculating Iowa dollars.

Marqusee also points out that another advantage of having more food produced locally is that the typical food supply on hand at grocers lasts for only three days. If we were to have a major disruption in our food chain—due to an energy crisis or terrorism event—we could face a food shortage right here in the heart of farm country. In 2010, the Maryland Legislature passed legislation similar to that proposed by Marqusee.[153]

In 2000, then Governor of Iowa Tom Vilsack, created the Iowa Food Policy Council by Executive Order. It was the first state food policy council in the nation. The 29-member council made policy recommendations for the governor and other state officials on a wide range of food issues, from recommending more purchases of local food by state-owned institutions to provisions for how Iowa could become a food-secure state where no one goes to bed hungry.

By the time the Iowa Food Policy's tenure expired in 2004, it made progress in a number of areas, including improving communication and cooperation among state agencies that work on food issues, bringing greater awareness of local food opportunities to farmers and consumers, and garnering more private and public resources to support the expansion of local food systems in Iowa. One of the noteworthy accomplishments of the pioneering work of the Iowa Food Policy Council was its role—and particularly the role of its chair, Neil Hamilton—in inspiring the creation of food policy councils in states and cities across the nation.

With the current growing public interest in local food and in the role food plays in our health and economy, the time is right for the revival of the Iowa Food Policy Council. The Council—with its broad base of stakeholder membership—could assess the current needs of Iowa's food system, survey and examine the many innovative food policy options now being proposed and implemented around the country, and make recommendations for policies and actions to strengthen Iowa's food system.

Currently, private efforts are under way to secure funding and authority for the Iowa Food Policy Council. I think that a good home for the Council is the Iowa Department of Agriculture and Land Stewardship, and that the secretary of agriculture should work with the Council to take its recommendations to the Iowa Legislature and governor's office.

35

Conclusion

We have looked at many challenges facing Iowa agriculture. To meet those challenges will require major changes for agriculture. Clearly, that will not happen overnight. It took many years for Iowa's agriculture to reach today's pinnacle of industrial production and fossil fuel dependency. We cannot expect it to change abruptly.

The important thing is that we first recognize the need to change direction, and then we begin the process of change in a direction that will position us for the future. Fortunately, we already have many innovative working models that are serving to show us what the future of Iowa agriculture could look like. We have models of how we can design and manage crop and livestock production systems that increase diversity and resilience on Iowa's landscape and protect and rebuild our natural resource base. We also have successful models for how we can make our farms more energy self-sufficient, how we can produce food for local communities, and how we can rebuild the economies of our rural communities.

Having these successful models in place can give us confidence that these successes can be multiplied across Iowa, and that with appropriate policy changes we can transform Iowa agriculture so it can thrive in a future in which oil exceeds $300 per barrel and weather extremes continue to increase. We can create an agriculture that is energy independent, and we can produce an abundant supply of healthy local food. In the process of transforming Iowa agriculture, we can help create a thriving Iowa economy and rebuild our rural communities.

Iowa can lead the nation in the transformation of agriculture so it will thrive in a new economy. Iowa can again be a shining jewel among agricultural states in a new era for agriculture. But it will require a clear vision for the future and steadfast action to get us there.

Author Biography

Francis Thicke was born in 1950 and grew up in a family of nine children on a diversified family farm near the town of LaCrescent, in southeastern Minnesota. The farm had dairy cows, hogs, chickens, sheep, and horses. Hay, oats, corn, and pasture crops were grown to feed the livestock. The family also had a very large garden and was nearly self-sufficient in their food needs. They canned and froze fruits and vegetables and butchered animals on the farm for home use.

During the 1960s, the farm became increasingly specialized as a dairy farm, with some hogs and chickens raised on the side. As a 4-H member, Francis showed a hog at the county fair each year. During high school years, Francis and his brothers got up at 4 a.m. to milk the cows so they could finish on time to catch the bus to school.

After high school, Francis attended Winona State College in Winona, Minnesota, graduating in 1972 with a B.A in music and philosophy. He began a graduate school program in orchestral trumpet performance at North Texas State University in Denton, Texas in 1973, but soon left to return to work on the family farm. Francis married Susan Noll in 1975.

In 1982, Francis began graduate studies in soil science. He completed his M.S. degree at the University of Minnesota in 1984 and his Ph.D. at the University of Illinois in 1988. Francis then began service as a soils specialist with the U.S. Department of Agriculture's Extension Service in Washington, D.C. He served at the USDA until 1992, during which time he was promoted to the position of National Program Leader for Soil Science for the USDA Extension Service.

In 1992, Francis and Susan moved to Fairfield, Iowa to return to farming. They took over operation of a small dairy farm that had recently begun processing and bottling milk on the farm. They converted the farm to certified organic production in 1993. As they diversified the dairy product line and expanded their market, they gradually increased the dairy herd size and eventually outgrew the small farm the dairy was on. In 1996, they purchased and moved to a 173-acre farm, where they built the dairy facility described in this book.

Over the years, several parcels of land that bordered their dairy farm came up for sale and the Thickes were able to expand their land base to 450 acres, which allowed them to continue to expand their herd and production of dairy products to meet the growing demand of their local community.

Currently, Francis and Susan, with help from five employees, milk about 80 cows and process their milk into fluid milk (whole, lowfat, and skim), cream, yogurt, and cheese, and market all their dairy products through grocery stores and restaurants in Fairfield.

Francis has long been active in leadership roles in organizations in his community, around Iowa and nationally. He has served on the Iowa Environmental Protection Commission and the Iowa Food Policy Council at the appointment of Governor Tom Vilsack and on the Iowa Organic Standards Board at the appointment of Governor Terry Branstad.

Other organizations Francis has served in include the USDA State Technical Committee, the Organic Farming Research Foundation Board, the Iowa State University Extension Advisory Committee, the Midwest Organic and Sustainable Education Services Board, the Scientific Congress on Organic Research Steering Committee, and the Consortium for Sustainable Agriculture Research and Education Governing Council.

Francis was invited to testify before the U.S. Senate Committee on Agriculture, Nutrition, and Forestry in 2007 to address the Research Title of the 2007 Farm Bill. He was also invited to testify before the U.S. Senate Subcommittee on Agriculture, Forestry, Conservation, and Rural Revitalization in 2004 to serve on a panel "Examining Conservation Programs of the 2002 Farm Bill."

Francis has received many awards for his service over the years, including the 2009 Spencer Award for Sustainable Agriculture from the Leopold Center for Sustainable Agriculture, the 2007 Sustainable Agriculture

Achievement Award from the Practical Farmers of Iowa, the "Friend of Extension" award from Iowa State University Extension Service in 2003, the "Outstanding Pasture Management" award from the Jefferson County Soil and Water Conservation District in 2001, and the "Steward of the Land" award from the Iowa Chapter of the Sierra Club in 2001.

In 2002, Francis was selected as a Fellow of the Food and Society Policy Fellows program, funded by the W. K. Kellogg Foundation. As a Food Policy Fellow for two years, Francis devoted half of his time to writing and speaking on issues related to food policy. Francis continues to make frequent keynote and workshop presentations on many facets of food and agriculture policy and on farming practices at conferences in Iowa and nationally.

References Cited

1   Ashton, T. S. The Industrial Revolution. London: Oxford University Press, 1969.

2   http://library.thinkquest.org/4132/info.htm

3   Kimbrell, Andrew, ed. *The Fatal Harvest Reader.* Washington: Island Press, 2002.

4   *"Number of crop and livestock enterprises produced for sale on Iowa farms, 1920-2002."* http://www.leopold.iastate.edu/pubs/staff/papers.htm.

5   Kahn, S. A., R. L. Mulvaney, T. R. Ellsworth and C. W. Boast. *The Myth of Nitrogen Fertilzation for Soil Carbon Sequestration.* J Environ Qual 36:1821-1832 2007.

6   http://en.wikipedia.org/wiki/List_of_time_periods

7   http://en.wikipedia.org/wiki/Information_Age

8   Cummins, Joe. *Glyphosate Resistance in Weeds.* Institute of Science in Society Report0 3/03/10. http://www.i-sis.org.uk/glyphosateResistanceTransgenicTreadmil.php

9   Govindarajulu, Purnima. *Literature review of impacts of glyphosate on amphibians: What risks can the silviculture use of this herbicide pose for amphibians in B.C?* British Columbia Ministry of Environment Wildlife Report No. R-28, June 2008.

10   de Vendomois J. S., Francois Roullier, Dominique Dellier, Gilles-Eric Seralini. *A Comparison of the Effects of Three GM Corn Varieties on Mammalian Health.* Int. J Biol Sce 2009; 5:706-726.

11   Smith, Jeffrey M. Genetic Roulette: *The Documented Health Risks of Genetically Engineered Foods.* 2007. Yes! Books, Fairfield IA.

12   Ostendorf, Martha. *Are We Shooting Ourselves In The Foot*

With A Silver Bullet? No-Till Farmer, March 2010.

13 http://www.rodaleinstitute.org/20080502/nf2

14 Rubin, Jeff. *Why Your World Is About To Get A Whole Lot Smaller.* Random House Canada., 2009.

15 http://www.epa.gov/region7/water/cafo/index.htm

16 factory farming. Dictionary.com. Dictionary.com's 21st Century Lexicon. Dictionary.com, LLC. http://dictionary.reference.com/browse/factory farming (accessed: April 03, 2010).

17 http://www.nffc.net/

18 Key, Nigel and William McBride. *The Changing Economics of U.S. Hog Production.* Economic Research Report No. (ERR-52). U.S. Department of Agriculture Economic Research Service, December, 2007.

19 Klingberg, Kevan. *Grazing Based Dairy Systems.* Understanding Nutrient & Sediment Loss at Breneman Farms – 1. Discovery Farms, University of Wisconsin-Madison.

20 Larson, Ben, James Kliebenstein, and Mark Honeyman. *Economics of Finishing Pigs in Hoop Structures and Confinement: a Summer Group.* ASL-R678. Iowa State University, Ames Iowa.

21 Landblom, D. G., W. W. Poland, B. Nelson, and E. Janzen. *An Economic Analysis of Swine Rearing Systems For North Dakota.* 2001 Annual Report. Dickinson Research Extension Center, North Dakota State University, Dickinson, ND.

22 Honeyman, Mark and Mike Duffy. *Iowa's Changing Swine Industry.* Iowa State University Animal Industry Report 2006. A.S. Leaflet R2158.

23 http://swineweb.com/usda-offers-loan-guidance-to-contract-pork-operations/

24 Hamilton, Scott. Testimony Before the United States Senate Committee on Agriculture, Nutrition, and Forestry. April 18, 2007. http://agriculture.senate.gov/Hearings/hearings.cfm?hearingid=2699&witnessId=6328.

25 Heffernan, William D. *Biotechnology and Mature Capitalism.* Presented at the 11th Annual Meeting of the National Agricultural Biotechnology Council. June, 1999. Lincoln Nebraska.

26 Heffernan, William and Mary Hendrickson. *Concentration of Agricultural Markets.* April 2007. http://www.nfu.org/wp-content/2007-heffernanreport.pdf.

27 Hirschfield, Peter. *Milking the Dairy Industry?* TimesArgus. com, August 2, 2009.

28 Johnson, Ron. *Dean Foods Sued by Justice Department for Antitrust Violations.* Jan. 29, 2010. Agri-View. Madison, WI.

29 http://www8.deanfoods.com/media/35708/fact_sheet_070709.pdf

30 http://www.monsanto.com/responsibility/sustainable-ag/default.asp

31 http://www.rio.iowa.gov/about_us/meetings/080508/04_conservation.pdf.

32 Bharati, L., K-H Lee, T. M. Isenhart, and R. C. Schultz. 2002. *Riparian zone soil-water infiltration under crops, pasture and established buffers.* Agroforestry Systems 56:249-257.

33 Battaglin, W. A. and D. A. Boolsby. *Nitrogen in the Mississippi Basin-Estimating Sources and Predicting Flux to the Gulf of Mexico.* USGS Fact Sheet 135-00, December 2000.

34 US Environmental Protection Agency. "Risk Management Evaluation for Concentrated Animal Feeding Operations." US EPA National Risk Management Laboratory. May 2004: 7.

35 *Preferential Flow of Manure in Tile Drainage.* eXtension April 27, 2010. http://www.extension.org/pages/Preferential_Flow_of_Manure_in_Tile_Drainage.

36 "*Threatening Iowa's Future: Iowa's Failure to Implement and Enforce the Clean Water Act for Livestock Operations.*" Environmental Integrity Project. May 2004. Available online at http://www.environmentalintegrity.org/pdf/publications/Report_Threatening_Iowa_Future.pdf.

37 *Draft Inventory of U.S. Greenhouse Gas Emissions and Sinks: 1990-2008.* March 2010. http://epa.gov/climatechange/emissions/usinventoryreport.html.

38 Paustian, Keith, John M. Antle, John Sheehan, Eldor A. Paul. *Agriculture's Role in Greenhouse Gas Mitigation.* September, 2006. Pew Center on Global Climate Change.

39   Davidson, Eric A. *The contribution of manure and fertilizer nitrogen to atmospheric nitrous oxide since 1860.* Nature Geoscience 2, 659-62 (2009).

40   *Draft Inventory of U.S. Greenhouse Gas Emissions and Sinks: 1990-2008.* March 2010. http://epa.gov/climatechange/emissions/usinventoryreport.html.

41   Ishler, Virginia. *Carbon, Methane Emissions and the Dairy Cow.* DAS 08-127. Penn State College of Agricultural Sciences.

42   Adam, David. *Move to cut methane emissions by changing cows' diet.* The Guardian, July 10, 2007. http://www.guardian.co.uk/science/2007/jul/10/ruralaffairs.climatechange.

43   *Draft Inventory of U.S. Greenhouse Gas Emissions and Sinks: 1990-2008.* March 2010. http://epa.gov/climatechange/emissions/usinventoryreport.html.

44   *Iowa Concentrated Animal Feeding Operations Air Quality Study* Final Report. February 2002. Iowa State University and The University of Iowa Study Group.

45   Ibid.

46   Ibid.

47   Ibid.

48   Ibid.

49   http://www.extension.iastate.edu/connection/2003ar/anr.html.

50   Heederid, Dick, T. Sigsgaard, PS Thorne, JN Kline, R Avery, JH Bonlokke, EA Chrischilles, JA Donsman, C Duchaine, SR Kirkhorn, K Kulhankova, and JA Merchant. *Health Effects of Airborne Exposures from Concentrated Animal Feeding Operations.* Environmental Health Perspectives. February 2007 115(2):298-302.

51   Schiffman, S., E. S. Miller, M. S. Suggs, and B. G. Graham BG. 1995. *The Effect of Environmental Odors Emanating from Commercial Swine Operations on the Mood of Nearby Residents.* Brain Research Bulletin 37(4):369-375.

52   Thu, K., K. Donham, R. Ziegenhorn, S. Reynolds, P. Thorne, P. Subramanian, P. Whitten, and J. Stookesberry. 1997. *A Control*

Study of the Physical and Mental Health of Residents Living Near a Large-Scale Swine Operation. Journal of Agricultural Safety and Health 3(1): 13-26.

53 Wing, S. and S. Wolf. 2000. *Intensive Livestock Operations, Health, and Quality of Life Among Eastern North Carolina Residents.* Environmental Health Perspectives 108(3):233-238.

54 Thu, Kendall M. Neighbor *Health and Large-scale Swine Production. National Ag Safety Database.* http://nasdonline.org/document/1829/d001764/neighbor-health-and-large-scale-swine-production.html.

55 Sigurdarson, S. T., J. N. Kline. *School Proximity of Concentrated Animal Feeding Operations and Prevalence of Asthma in Students.* CHEST June 2006 vol. 129 no.6 1486-1491.

56 Sneeringer, Stacy. *Does Animal Feeding Operation Pollution Hurt Public Health? A National Longitudinal Study of Health Externalities Identified by Geographic Shifts in Livestock Production.* American Journal of Agricultural Economics. 2009 91: 124-137.

57 http://tobaccodocuments.org/landman/332506.html.

58 Kovac, M. *Humane Society drops animal-care issue from ballot Group negotiates agreement with Strickland, farm bureau.* July 6, 2010. Recordpub.com. http://www.recordpub.com/news/article/4854732

59 National Park Service, U.S. Department of the Interior. http://www.nps.gov/thro/naturescience/bison-buffalo.htm.

60 National Agricultural Statistics Service, U.S. Department of Agriculture. http://www.nass.usda.gov/QuickStats/index2.jsp.

61 The Stockman Grass Farmer. P.O Box 9607 Jackson, MS 39286. http://stockmangrassfarmer.net/.

62 Clancy, K. 2006. Greener Pastures: *How Grass-Fed Beef and Milk Contribute to Healthier Eating.* Union of Concerned Scientists. Available at www.ucsusa.org.

63 Duffy, Mike, Matt Liebman, Ken Pecinovsky. *Organic vs. Conventional Farming Systems.* ISRF02-13. Iowa State University Northeast Research and Demonstration Farm. http://www.ag.iastate.edu/farms/02reports/ne/OrganicConvSystems.pdf.

64 Catherine Badgleya, Jeremy Moghtader, Eileen Quintero,

Emily Zakem, M. Jahi Chappell, Katia Avilés-Vázquez, Andrea Samulonand Ivette Perfecto. *Organic agriculture and the world food supply.* Renewable Agriculture and Food Systems (2007), 22: 86-108 Cambridge University Press.

65 Hine, Rachael and Jules Pretty. *Organic Agriculture and Food Security in Africa.* UNCTAD/DITC/TED/2007/15 2008. United Nations Conference on Trade and Development, United Nations Environment Programme.

66 *Agriculture at a Crossroads. International Assessment of Agricultural Knowledge, Science and Technology for Development.* April, 2008. http://www.agassessment.org.

67 *No Relief in Sight for High Fertilizer Prices.* Lancaster Farming, May 9, 2008. http://lancasterfarming.com/node/1246.

68 *Farm Income and Costs: 2010 Farm Sector Income Forecast.* USDA-ERS. http://www.ers.usda.gov/Briefing/FarmIncome/nationalestimates.htm.

69 Rubin, Jeff. *Why Your World is About to Get a Whole Lot Smaller.* 2009. Random House Canada.

70 Brown, Lester R. *Plan B 3.0, 2008.* W. W. Norton and Company, Inc., London.

71 The Joint Operating Environment 2010. United States Joint Forces Command. http://www.peakoil.net/files/JOE2010.pdf.

72 U. S. Agriculture and Forestry Greenhouse Gas Inventory: 1990-2005. http://www.usda.gov/oce/global_change/AFGGInventory1990_2005.htm.

73 Cox, C. and A. Hug. *Driving under the influence: Corn ethanol & energy security.* June 2010. Environmental Working Group.

74 *Light-Duty Automotive Technology and Fuel Economy Trends; 1975 Through 2008.* EPA420-S-08-003. http://www.epa.gov/oms/cert/mpg/fetrends/420s08003.pdf.

75 McKibben, Bill. Washington Post. May 27, 2006. http://www.washingtonpost.com/wp-dyn/content/article/2006/05/26/AR2006052601549.html.

76 http://frwebgate.access.gpo.gov/cgi-bin/getdoc.cgi?dbname=110_cong_bills&docid=f:h6enr.txt.pdf.

77   *Miscanthus for Biofuel Production*. Heaton, E. A., N. Boersma, J. D. Caveny, T. B. Voigt, and F. G. Dohelman. eXtension, March 16, 2010. http://www.extension.org/pages/Miscanthus_for_Biofuel_Production.

78   Summary Report, 2007 National Resource Inventory. USDA-NRCS. http://www.nrcs.usda.gov/technical/NRI/2007/2007_NRI_Summary.pdf.

79   USDA-NASS. http://www.nass.usda.gov/.

80   Ibid.

81   Randall,G. W., D. R. Huggins, M. P. Russelle, D. J. Fuchs, W. W. Nelson and J. L. Anderson. *Nitrate Losses through Subsurface Tile Drainage in Conservation Reserve Program, Alfalfa, and Row Crop Systems*. Journal of Environmental Quality 26:1240-1247 (1997).

82   Heaton, E. A., F. G. Dohlman, and S. P. Long. *Seasonal nitrogen dynamics of Miscanthus x Giganteus and Panicum virgatum*. GBC Bioenergy (2009) 1, 297-307 doi: 10:1111/j.1957-1707.2009.01022.x

83   http://www.iowarfa.org/ethanol_facts.php.

84   Schmer, M. R., Vogel, K. P., Mitchell, R. B. & Perrin, R. K. *"Net energy of cellulosic ethanol from switchgrass"* Proc. Natl. Acad. Sci. USA 105, 464-469 (2008).

85   Heaton, E. A.[1], Nboersma, J. D. Caveny, T. B. Voigt and F. G. Dohleman. *Miscanthus for Biofuel Production*. March 16, 2010. eXtension. http://www.extension.org/pages/Miscanthus_for_Biofuel_Production.

86   De Decker, Kris. 2010. *Wood Gas Vehicles*: Firewood in the tank. Post Carbon Institute. http://www.energybulletin.net/node/51237.

87   Gaunt, J. L. and J. Lehmann. *Energy Balance and Emissions Associated with Biochar Sequestration and Pyrolysis Bioenergy Production*. Environ. Sci. Technol. 2008. 42, 4152-4158.

88   Sadaka, S. and A. A. Boateng. *Pyrolysis and Bio-Oil*. FSA1052, University of Arkansas Division of Agriculture.

89   Holmgren, J., R. Bain, P. Nair, R. Marinangeli, D Elliot. *Converting Pyrolysis Oils to Renewable Transport Fuels: Processing*

Challenges & Opportunities. AM-08-81. National Petrochemical
& Refiners Association Annual Meeting, March 9-11, 2008.

90   http://www.agri-therm.com/index.htm.

91   Brown, R. and J. Homgren. *Fast Pyrolysis and Bio-Oil
Upgrading.* http://www.ars.usda.gov/sp2UserFiles/Program/307/
biomasstoDiesel/RobertBrown&JenniferHolmgrenpresentationsl
ides.pdf.

92   http://en.wikipedia.org/wiki/Biochar.

93   Bruges, J. 2009. *The Biochar Debate.* Chelsea Green Publish-
ing.

94   Weil, R. R. and F. Magdoff. 2004. *Significance of Soil Organic
Matter to Soil Quality and Health.* In Soil Organic Matter in
Sustainable Agriculture. Ed. By F. Magdoff and R. R. Weil.

95   *Breaking Land: the Loss of Organic Matter.* March 30, 2010.
Soil Quality for Environmental Health. http://soilquality.org/
history/history_om_loss.html.

96   Gaunt, J. L. and J. Lehmann. *Energy Balance and Emissions
Associated with Biochar Sequestration and Pyrolysis Bioenergy
Production.* Environ. Sci. Technol. 2008. 42, 4152-4158.

97   Howell, K. *Is Algae the Biofuel of the Future?* Scientific
American. April 28, 2009.

98   Zenk, P. *On-Farm Ethanol.* Hay and Forage Grower. Novem-
ber2008.

99   Cox, T. S., J. D. Glover, D. L. Van Tassel, C. M. Cox, and
L. R. DeHann. *Prospects for developing perennial plants.* Biosci-
ence2006, Vol. 56, No. 8, pp 649 -659. ,

100 Osterberg, D. and T. Galluzzo. *Think Wind Power, Think
'Iowa.'* The Iowa Policy Project. March, 2010. http://www.iowapol-
icyproject.org/2010docs/100303-IPP-wind.pdf.

101 Osterberg, D. and T. Galluzzo. *Think Wind Power, Think
'Iowa.'* The Iowa Policy Project. March, 2010. http://www.iowapol-
icyproject.org/2010docs/100303-IPP-wind.pdf.

102 Galbraith, K. *Europe's Way of Encouraging Solar Power Ar-
rives in the U.S.* New York Times, March 12, 2009. http://www.
nytimes.com/2009/03/13/business/energy-environment/13solar.
html.

103 Osterberg, D. and T. Galluzzo. *Think Wind Power, Think 'Iowa.'* The Iowa Policy Project. March, 2010. http://www.iowapolicyproject.org/2010docs/100303-IPP-wind.pdf.

104 Graham-Rowe, D. The Guardian, June 19, 2009. http://www.guardian.co.uk/environment/2009/jun/19/denmark-wind-electric-cars.

105 Fairley, P. *Electric-Car Maker Touts 10-Minute Fill-up.* IEEE Spectrum, November, 2009. http://spectrum.ieee.org/green-tech/advanced-cars/electriccar-maker-touts-10minute-fillup.

106 Globally-Unique Ammonia Production. University of Minnesota-Morris. http://renewables.morris.umn.edu/wind/ammonia/.

107 Stender, C. *Nitrogen Source Could Become as Close as the Nearest Wind Turbine.* AgriNews, 12/1/09. http://www.agrinews.com/nitrogen/source/could/become/as/close/as/the/nearest/wind/turbine/story-1060.html.

108 http://www.agrinews.com/nitrogen/source/could/become/as/close/as/the/nearest/wind/turbine/story-1060.html.

109 http://en.wikipedia.org/wiki/Compressed-air_engine.

110 Lampton, C. *How the Air Car Works.* http://auto.howstuffworks.com/fuel-efficiency/vehicles/air-car.htm.

111 http://www.landinstitute.org/vnews/display.v/ART/2007/03/15/45facffb6ccd6.

112 Fundamentals *of a Sustainable U.S. Biofuels Policy.* Baker Institute Policy Report Number 43, January 2010. http://www.rice.edu/ Car Works. http://auto.howstuffworks.com/fuel-efficiency/vehicles/air-car.htm.energy/publications/PolicyReports/study_43.pdf.

113 http://www.frac.org/html/hunger_in_the_us/hunger_index.html.

114 http://en.wikipedia.org/wiki/Iowa.

115 http://frac.org/data/.

116 Tagtow, A. *A vision for "Good Food" for Iowa.* April 2008. A Public Health Primer.

117 http://www.leopold.iastate.edu/pubs/staff/files/farm_enter-

prises_1204.pdf.

118 *Is it time to grow a victory garden? Feb. 23. 2009.* eXtension. http://www.extension.org/pages/Is_it_Time_to_Grow_a_Victory_Garden percent3F

119 *The 100-Mile Diet: Is it healthier and safer for the population?* Current Issues. 2010. Dieticians of Canada.

120 Dumas Y, M. Dadomo, G. Di Lucca, P. Grolier. Review. *Effects of environmental factors and agricultural techniques on antioxidant content of tomatoes.* J Sci Food Agric. 2003; 83: 369–382.

121 Worthington V. Nutritional quality of organic versus conventional fruits, vegetables, and grains. J Altern Complement Med. 2001; 7(2): 161–173.

122 Halweil B. Still No Free Lunch: Nutrient levels in U.S. food supply eroded by pursuit of high yields. Critical Issues Report. The Organic Center. September 2007.

123 Harvard Medical School, Center For Health and the Global Environment, *Healthy and Sustainable Food. Is Local More Nutritious? It Depends.* 2007 [cited 2009 24 Sept]. Available from: http://chge.med.harvard.edu/programs/food/nutrition.html.

124 Lee, S. K., Kader, A. A. *Preharvest and postharvest factors influencing vitamin C content of horticultural crops.* Postharvest Biol Technol. 2000; 20: 207–220.

125 Harvard Medical School, Center For Health and the Global Environment, *Healthy and Sustainable Food. Is Local More Nutritious? It Depends.* 2007 [cited 2009 24 Sept]. Available from: http://chge.med.harvard.edu/programs/food/nutrition.html.

126 Halweil B. *Still No Free Lunch: Nutrient levels in U.S. food supply eroded by pursuit of high yields.* Critical Issues Report. The Organic Center. September 2007.

127 Pirog, Rich, Timothy Van Pelt, Kamyar Enshayan, and Ellen Cook. 2001. *Food, Fuel, and Freeways: An Iowa Perspective on How Far Food Travels, Fuel Usage, and Greenhouse Gas Emissions.* The Leopold Center for Sustainable Agriculture, June. Available at http://www.leopold.iastate.edu/pubs/staff/ppp/food_mil.pdf.

128 Swenson, D. *The Economic Impacts of Increased Fruit and*

Vegetable Production and Consumption in Iowa: Phase II. May 2006. Leopold Center for Sustainable Agriculture. http://www. leopold.iastate.edu/pubs/staff/files/health_0606.pdf.

129 Swenson, D. *Selected Measures of the Economic Values of Increased Fruit and Vegetable Production and Consumption in the Upper Midwest.* Leopold Center for Sustainable Agriculture. http://www.leopold.iastate.edu/research/marketing_files/Midwest_032910.pdf

130 http://www.spinfarming.com/whatsSpin/.

131 http://www.crcworks.org/?submit=rural.

132 http://www.crcworks.org/lea/blackhawksum06.pdf.

133 U.S. Department of Health and Human Services. National Health Expenditure Data. http://www.cms.gov/National-HealthExpendData/02_NationalHealthAccountsHistorical. asp#TopOfPage.

134 *Food Expenditures by Families and Individuals as a Share of Personal Disposable Income.* U.S. Department of Agriculture-Economic Research Service. http://www.ers.usda.gov/Briefing/CPIFoodAndExpenditures/Data/table7.htm.

135 Pollan, M. The Food Movement, Rising. New York Review of Books. http://www.nybooks.com/articles/archives/2010/jun/10/food-movement-rising/?page=1.

136 Economic Costs of Diabetes in the U.S. in 2007. American Diabetes Association. http://care.diabetesjournals.org/content/31/3/596.full.

137 *Researchers Verify Link Between Type 2 Diabetes And Diet.* Medical News Today. July 30, 2008. http://www.medicalnewstoday.com/articles/116513.php.

138 Babey, S, M. Jones, H. Yu and H. Goldstein. *Bubbling Over: Soda Consumption and Its Link to Obesity in California.* September, 2009. UCLA Center for Health Policy Research. http://www.healthpolicy.ucla.edu/pubs/Publication.aspx?pubID=375.

139 Edelson, E. *Increasing Soda Consumption Fuels Rise in Diabetes, Heart Disease.* http://www.medicinenet.com/script/main/art.asp?articlekey=114184.

140 Reinberg, S. ABC News/Health. July 27, 2009. http://abcnews.

go.com/Health/Healthday/story?id=8184975&page=1.

141 Khan, L. K., K. Sobush, D. keener, K. Goodman, A. Lowry, J. Kakietek, and S. Zaro. *Recommended Community Strategies and Measurements to Prevent Obesity in the United States.* July 24, 2009 /58(RRo7); 1-26. CDC Recommendations and Reports.

142 Pirog, R. *Checking the food odometer: Comparing food miles for local versus conventional produce sales to Iowa institutions.* Leopold Center for Sustainable Agriculture. http://www.leopold. iastate.edu/pubs/staff/files/food_travel072103.pdf.

143 Rubin, J. *Why Your World Is About To Get A Whole Lot Smaller.* 2009. Random House Canada.

144 Otto, D. *2009 Farmers Market Economic Impact Survey.* Iowa Department of Agriculture.

145 *Community Supported Agriculture.* Alternative Farming Systems Information Center. USDA-National Agricultural Library. http://www.nal.usda.gov/afsic/pubs/csa/csa.shtml.

146 http://www.iowafood.org.

147 http://www.leopold.iastate.edu/research/marketing_files/ vcp.html.

148 Dunn, K. *Unheated Greenhouse Project Offers Growers Hopes of Profitability From Longer Growing Season.* Sept. 26, 2006. Cornell University Chronicle Online. http://www.news. cornell.edu/stories/Sept06/tunnel.tomatoes.kd.html.

149 Raz, G. *Farmers Markets: Fresh, Local, Government Approved.* National Public Radio. October 4, 2009. http://www.npr. org/templates/story/story.php?storyId=113484871.

150 Klinkenborg, V. Good *News From Iowa.* New York Times, February 9, 2009. http://www.nytimes.com/2009/02/10/ opinion/10tue4.html.

151 http://www.leopold.iastate.edu/resources/guide/guide.pdf.

152 http://www.woodburyorganics.com/Woodbury_Organics/ Main_files/LFFSA percent20v2.1.pdf.

153 http://www.woodburyorganics.com/Woodbury_Organics/ Main.html